GROVE PRESS MODERN DRAMATISTS

Grove Press Modern Dramatists
Series Editors: *Bruce King* and *Adele King*

Published titles

Eugene Benson, *J. M. Synge*

Normand Berlin, *Eugene O'Neill*

Neil Carson, *Arthur Miller*

Ruby Cohn, *New American Dramatists, 1960–1980*

Bernard F. Dukore, *Harold Pinter*

Frances Gray, *John Arden*

Julian Hilton, *Georg Büchner*

Charles R. Lyons, *Samuel Beckett*

Susan Bassnett-McGuire, *Luigi Pirandello*

Leonard C. Pronko, *Eugène Labiche and Georges Feydeau*

Theodore Shank, *American Alternative Theatre*

Nick Worrall, *Nikolai Gogol and Ivan Turgenev*

Further titles in preparation

GROVE PRESS MODERN DRAMATISTS

SAMUEL BECKETT

Charles R. Lyons
Professor of Drama and Comparative Literature
Stanford University

Grove Press, Inc., New York

First published in 1983 by
THE MACMILLAN PRESS LTD.
London and Basingstoke

First Hardcover Edition 1983
First Printing 1983
ISBN: 0-394-53231-7
Library of Congress Catalog Card Number: 82-47987

First Evergreen Edition 1983
First Printing 1983
ISBN: 0-394-62411-4
Library of Congress Catalog Card Number: 82-47987

Library of Congress Cataloging in Publication Data

Lyons, Charles R.
    Samuel Beckett.

    (Grove Press modern dramatists)
    Bibliography: p.
    Includes index.
    1. Beckett, Samuel, 1906-   --Criticism and
interpretation. I. Title. II. Series.
PR6003.E282Z7716 1983   848'.91409   82-25137
ISBN 0-394-53231-7
ISBN 0-394-62411-4 (pbk.)

Printed in the United States of America

GROVE PRESS, INC., 196 West Houston Street,
New York, N.Y., 10014

    5 4 3 2 1

Contents

v

List of Plates

1. *En Attendant Godot*, at the Theatre de Babylone, Paris in 1953, with Jean Martin and Roger Blin. Photo: Lipnitzki-Viollet.
2. *Waiting for Godot*, at the Royal Court Theatre, London in 1964 with Nicol Williamson and Alfred Lynch. Photo: Zoe Dominic.
3. *Fin de Partie*, at the Studio Champs Elysees, Paris 1957 with Roger Blin and Jean Martin. Photo: Lipnitzki-Viollet.
4. *Endgame* at the Cherry Lane Theatre, New York, 1958, with Lester Rawlins and Alun Epstein. Photo: Alix Jeffry/Harvard Theatre Collection.
5. *Endgame* at the Cherry Lane Theatre. New York in 1958 with P. J. Kelly as Nagg. Photo: Alix Jeffry/Harvard Theatre Collection.
6. *Play* at the Old Vic Theatre, London in 1964. Billie Whitelaw, Robert Stephens, Rosemary Harris. Photo: Zoe Dominic.
7. *Krapp's Last Tape* at the Forum Theatre, New York 1972. Hume Cronyn as Krapp. Photo: Martha Swope.
8. *Happy Days* at the Royal Court Theatre, London 1974. Peter Hall directing Peggy Ashcroft. Photo: Zoe Dominic.
9. *Happy Days* at the Royal Court Theatre, London 1979. Billie Whitelaw. Photo: Donald Cooper.
10. *Rockaby* at the Centre for Theatre Research in Buffalo, New York in 1981 Billie Whitelaw. Photo: Suzanne Donelly Jenkins.

Editors' Preface

The *Grove Press Modern Dramatists* is an international series of introductions to major and significant nineteenth- and twentieth-century dramatists, movements and new forms of drama in Europe, Great Britain, America and new nations such as Nigeria and Trinidad. Besides new studies of great and influential dramatists of the past, the series includes volumes on contemporary authors, recent trends in the theatre and on many dramatists, such as writers of farce, who have created theatre 'classics' while being neglected by literary criticism. The volumes in the series devoted to individual dramatists include a biography, a survey of the plays, and detailed analysis of the most significant plays, along with discussion, where relevant of the political, social, historical and theatrical context. The authors of the volumes, who are involved with theatre as playwrights, directors, actors, teachers and critics, are concerned with the plays as theatre and discuss such matters as performance, character interpretation and staging, along with themes and contexts.

Editors' Preface

Grove Press Modern Dramatists are written for people interested in modern theatre who prefer concise, intelligent studies of drama and dramatists, without jargon and an excess of footnotes.

BRUCE KING
ADELE KING

For Jamie

Acknowledgements

The author and publishers are grateful to the following copyright holders for permission to quote from the works of Samuel Beckett:

John Calder (Publishers) Ltd. for extracts from the novels *Molloy*, *Malone Dies* and *The Unnamable*.

Faber and Faber Ltd. for extracts from the plays *Waiting for Godot*, *Endgame*, *All that Fall*, *Krapp's Last Tape*, *Happy Days*, *Embers*, *Play* (including *Words and Music* and *Cascando*), *That Time and Not I*, *Film*, *Footfalls*, *Three Occasional Pieces* (including *A Piece of Monologue* and *Rockaby*).

GROVE PRESS MODERN DRAMATISTS

1
Introduction

Samuel Beckett has been a famous literary figure since the international success of *Waiting for Godot*. In 1969, sixteen years after this 'tragicomedy' confounded its first audience, he was awarded the Nobel Prize for Literature. Beckett, however, has persistently refused to become a public person, and he guards the details of his private life carefully. His own writing is his most reliable biography in the sense that it documents the working life of a keenly perceptive, widely read and profoundly speculative author. Beckett has devoted his life to writing; for many years he lived on a restricted income, following his own direction as a writer despite the difficulties he encountered finding publishers for his work. In the radio play, *Cascando*, written in 1962, he represents the public and private personalities of a writer as two distinct characters. The private self speaks continuously in a state of compulsive fictionalising; the writer's ego makes his speech audible to the public, opening and closing the sound of the narrative. This ego complains that the public does not think that his writing is his life. He states that 'they', his readers or his critics, claim 'That is not his life, he does not live on that.' He counters: 'I have lived on it . . . pretty long. Long enough.'[1] If we knew no details of Beckett's biography, we would still have the sequence of his texts, the words that form the principal images and conceptual schemes with which he perceives his experience.

Samuel Barclay Beckett was born into an upper-middle-class Protestant family in Foxrock, a suburb south of Dublin, in 1906. He studied French and Italian at Trinity College and earned a bachelor of arts degree in 1927. In 1928 he went to the École Normale Supérieure in Paris as one of two *lecteurs d'anglais*. In Paris he joined the band of disciples that surrounded James Joyce, the author of *Ulysses* and a fellow Irishman. The ferment and excitement stimulated by Joyce's current project, the unusual text that would become *Finnegan's Wake*, captured Beckett's imagination, and Joyce asked him to contribute to a collection of essays written by his followers to defend their master's work. His essay, Beckett's first published work, traces Joyce's use of key Italian writers: 'Dante . . . Bruno. Vico . . . Joyce' is the leading article in the twelve essays that comprise *Our Exagmination Round his Factification for Incamination of Work in Progress.*

The twenty-three-year-old Samuel Beckett discusses ideas in this essay that continue to inform his writing. He claims the author's right to create an opaque text that is difficult for the reader to comprehend, and he argues against the division of form and content: 'The form that is an arbitrary and independent phenomenon can fulfill no higher function than that of a stimulus for a tertiary or quartenary conditioned reflex of dribbling comprehension.' The polemic *Exagmination* was published in 1929, the same year in which Eugene Jolas' journal, *transition*, offered its readers the first piece of Beckett's fiction to appear in print. The short story, 'Assumption', and a reprint of the Joyce essay are included in the same issue. This little magazine, which was an important vehicle of the *avant-garde*, continued to publish Beckett's work when conventional publishers rejected his manuscripts.

Beckett's admiration for the work of James Joyce obviously influenced his writing, and the impact of the older writer upon the younger provides scholars with rich material for discussion. The exuberant language of *Murphy*, Beckett's first novel, shows the influence of his master's style, but the simple prose spoken by the two tramps in *Waiting for Godot* shows the distance Beckett has travelled from the sound of his early mentor. Beckett's work soon begins to mark his differences from Joyce. Whereas the author of *Finnegan's Wake* celebrates language and the special worlds it creates, Beckett consistently questions the power of language to signify, demonstrating a keen scepticism about the possibility that words can sustain a concept of reality for any length of time.

The economy of language in *Godot*, which Beckett wrote originally in French as *En attendant Godot*, illustrates the progressive sparseness of Beckett's use of words. A study of his manuscripts reveals his painstaking processes of reduction, intensification and simplification. Beckett claims that he writes in French to avoid indulging in 'style',[2] and the discipline of this practice seems to be a self-conscious effort to restrain and confine his language.

Samuel Beckett's two years in Paris at the École Normale were extremely active ones. He continued his study of Descartes, whose philosophy had already influenced him profoundly. Descartes bases his belief in the existence of God on the notion that a finite mind could not originate the idea of the infinite. While Beckett's scepticism would not allow him to accept that argument, Descartes' emphasis upon the mind as the principal field of scientific investigation aligns with Beckett's relentless exploration of the processes of consciousness. Descartes' doubts about the accuracy of the concept of external reality that we gain from sense-perception provided Beckett with a philosophical scheme that he has used consistently in his fiction and drama: the image of a mind, alienated from its body, that questions the reality of the world it inhabits and, at the same time, studies itself to question the validity of its reasoning. Beckett employed the figure of Descartes parodistically as the subject of 'Whoroscope', an erudite poem that he wrote for a competition sponsored by Nancy Cunard and the Hours Press. He won the prize, and the esoteric one hundred lines became his first independently published work in a special edition printed in 1930.

While Beckett taught in Paris, he also completed a critical study of Marcel Proust. This monograph, which had been commissioned by Chatto and Windus for the Dolphin series, examines the novelist's notions of the insubstantiality of personality and analyses his concepts of time, memory and habit in discussions that illuminate both Proust and the writing of Beckett himself. *Proust* is less polemic than the essay on Joyce, but it continues his attack on realism in its praise of Proust's method of representing the mediation of objects in consciousness. He defends Proust's impressionism: 'By his impressionism I mean his non-logical statement of phenomena in the order and exactitude of their perception, before they have been distorted into intelligibility in order to be forced into a chain of cause and effect.'

Introduction

Proust was published in 1931 after Beckett had returned to Trinity College to assume a teaching post and to complete a master's degree. He appeared to be well started on a conventional academic career. Beckett, however, found it impossible to continue teaching, and at Easter 1932 he fled to Europe and resigned from Trinity by letter. He spent a troubled two years in London, and the scenes he encountered there appear in *Murphy*, which was not published until 1938. Incorporating parts of a novel he had begun in Paris, Beckett wrote a series of short stories, *More Pricks than Kicks*, that feature a hero named after Dante's slothful Belacqua and scenes that appear to offer ironic variations on Joyce's *Dubliners*. *Echo's Bones*, a sequence of thirteen poems, followed in 1935.

In October 1936, Samuel Beckett moved permanently to Paris. In 1937 he took a seventh-floor apartment where he made his home until 1961. In 1938 he was stabbed in a bizarre street incident and came close to death. About this time he met his wife, Suzanne Deschevaux-Dumesnil. Beckett left Paris in June 1940, ahead of the advancing German Army. He returned in October to join the Resistance, preparing information on troop movements for microfilming. The identity of his group was exposed by a colleague under torture, but Beckett was warned by the wife of another friend and he escaped shortly before he would have been apprehended. Like Vladimir and Estragon, Beckett worked in the Vaucluse, near Avignon, as an agricultural worker, finishing the text of his second novel, *Watt*, in his free time. In 1945 he returned to Ireland and enlisted in the Red Cross as a volunteer. For six months he worked at the Irish Red Cross Hospital in Saint Lo. Beckett then returned to Paris and once again took up residence in his old apartment.

He had written a sequence of thirteen poems in French

in 1939, and after the war he began to write fiction in that language – a brief novel, *Mercier et Camier*, and four stories, all of which he did not release for publication until after the success of his later work. He interrupted work on his trilogy of novels – *Molloy, Malone Dies* and *The Unnamable* – to write *Éleuthéria*, an unpublished play, after completing the first novel, and *Godot* after finishing the second. He continued to have difficulty finding a willing publisher, but late in 1950 he established a relationship with Les Editions de Minuit that led to the publication of the trilogy, *Godot* and *Watt*. About the same time Roger Blin, the fine actor and director, became interested in the scripts of both *Éleuthéria* and *Godot*. Blin eventually selected *Godot* for production because its fewer characters and simpler set made it cheaper to mount; he produced the play in January 1953. After years of penury the success of *Godot* and his subsequent works brought Beckett and his wife, Suzanne, the security of an ample income; he was able to buy a flat in Montparnasse and, as well, to build a small country house in Ussy. Beckett divides his time between the two homes, maintaining a secluded life and protecting himself, as much as possible, from the public intrusions that being a major literary figure brings.

Continuing to write drama and fiction in both English and French, Beckett works as self-translator from one language to the other. After the success of *Godot* he published a series of dramatic works including: *Fin de partie* [*Endgame*] in 1957; *All that Fall*, a radio play in 1957; *Krapp's Last Tape* in 1958; *Embers*, a radio play, in 1959; *Happy Days* in 1961; *Words and Music* and *Cascando*, two plays for radio, in 1964, broadcast in 1962 and 1963; *Play* in 1964; a film titled *Film* in 1964; *Eh Joe*, a television play, in 1967; *Come and Go* in 1967; *Not I* in

1973; *That Time* and *Footfalls* in 1976, *A Piece of Monologue* in 1979; and *Rockaby* and *Ohio Impromptu* in 1981.

After the trilogy his fiction includes: *Comment C'est* [*How It Is*] in 1961; *Imagination morte Imaginez* [*Imagination Dead Imagine*] in 1965; *Le Depeupleur* [*The Lost Ones*] in 1971; *Assez* [*Enough*] and *Bing* in 1966; *Sans* [*Lessness*] in 1969; *Pour finir encore et autres foirades* [*Fizzles*] in 1976; *Compagnie* [*Company*] in 1980.

While Beckett continues to fascinate readers and spectators with radically experimental works of fiction and drama, his principal subject remains the same, an extrapolation of Descartes' model: the consciousness of an ageing person grappling with his clouded perception of the space he inhabits, attempting to reconcile images of the past that revolve in his imagination, questioning his own identity and the authenticity of his existence. Beckett continually reconstitutes this image in new forms, and each text develops a structural scheme that is more economical than its predecessor. In his recent work of prose fiction, *Company*, he writes of an old man who lies on his back in a dark space and listens to a voice speaking. The words of the text represent the thought processes of the listener. As readers we do not encounter the speaker's words directly; we learn of the content of the speech only through the report of the old man. He is, however, not certain that the voice addresses him. Although the speech refers to certain details of the listener's life, in words that suggest the voice talks to him, the old man confronts a basic epistemological question. He cannot verify the details of his immediate experience sufficiently to assume, unequivocally, that the speaker addresses him or, for that matter, speaks the truth if he does. The details that the speaker uses form the images in which the old man perceives himself, but the

7

listener's doubt creates an irredeemable gap between his consciousness and those words.

The protagonists of Beckett's recent plays are also listeners. In *Rockaby* a woman rocks in a chair listening to her recorded voice rehearse her failure to find 'another like herself'. In *Ohio Impromptu* the subject of the drama sits at a table while his double sits opposite reading to him from a book that tells the story of a man sitting at a table opposite his double who reads to him from a book. The story he reads, however, reports that the reader is making his last call, suggesting that this reading is the final one. The only identity the old man has is the one sustained by the text that the other man reads; when that reading ends, of course, his presence dissolves.

Beckett's first novel, which is a richly comic and elaborately detailed narrative, tells the story of Murphy's movement towards an absolute isolation, a state of being in which he is able to close off his vision of himself. In a late stage of his progress toward that goal, Murphy finds satisfaction in his work as an attendant in an asylum, particularly in his relationship with a peculiar patient with the punning name of Endon. He is delighted to discover that Endon's solipsistic world is so complete that the man cannot see him even though his eyes are fixed upon the attendant:

> . . . his fingers, his lips, nose and forehead almost touching Mr. Endon's, seeing himself stigmatised in those eyes that did not see him, Murphy heard words demanding so strongly to be spoken that he spoke them, right into Mr. Endon's face, Murphy who did not speak at all in the ordinary way unless spoken to, and not always even then.
>
> 'the last at last seen of him

8

himself unseen by him
and of himself'
A rest,
   'the last Mr. Murphy saw of Mr. Endon was Mr.
Murphy unseen by Mr. Endon. This was also the last
Murphy saw of Murphy.'[3]

The experience of being unseen by Mr Endon allows
Murphy to complete the process of erasing himself from
his own field of perception, disciplining his mind to accept
his suicide. Beckett creates the character of Murphy and
then represents his disappearance, both to himself and to
the readers. This paradigm of establishing and dissolving
images of the self persists throughout Beckett's writing.
   In the trilogy of novels, which Beckett wrote in the same
period in which he composed *Godot*, he developed a series
of protagonists who are writers and whose writing
constitutes the text of the novels. *Molloy* and *Malone Dies*
pretend to be the memoirs of their heroes, Molloy, Moran
and Malone; but the protagonist of the third novel,
Mahood, suggests that he has invented the other characters
within his imagination. In that way Beckett destroys the
fiction he has created in the first two novels and dissolves
the fictional presence of Molloy, Moran and Malone.
   Theatrical performance depends upon the concrete
presence of the human actor; when the actor appears
before the audience, both his character and the scene he
inhabits assume a strong sense of objective reality.
Beckett's desire to write for the theatre poses a paradox.
While his fiction works to dissolve the image of character,
he elects to work in an aesthetic medium, the theatre, that
depends upon the actual presence of a human actor. The
stability of that objective image of reality constitutes an
aesthetic problem that Beckett sets out to explore. The

experimentation that informs all the plays from *Waiting for Godot* to *Ohio Impromptu* reveals the playwright's deliberate manipulation of the basic theatrical conventions of representing characters in space and time. Beckett develops strategies to present an illusion of character, held in the physical presence of the actor, and then dissolves the spectator's belief in the authenticity of that human image. When Vladimir questions the young boy who comes at the end of each act in *Godot* to deliver his master's message, the child denies that he has been there before and seen the two tramps. We know that his second denial is false, because we have seen him with Vladimir and Estragon in the first act. However, we recognise the possibility that, for some reason, the images of these two old men may not sustain themselves in the child's perception. If he is to appear again, he may encounter the two without memory of a previous encounter. In *Endgame* Beckett structures his drama so that his spectators are unsure when Hamm performs himself and when he assumes a role. Hamm is a powerful and dynamic theatrical presence, but our persistent speculation and doubt about the authenticity of his performance diminishes our sense of his presence as a human image. *Krapp's Last Tape* isolates the memories of the character in a tape-recording made thirty years before the performance and presents the immediate image of the character as an old man incapable of assimilating those memories at any meaningful level of perception. The voice on the tape establishes the image of character; the physical presence of the old man marks the absence of that vital figure. In *Happy Days* Beckett presents the character of a middle-aged woman who is gradually being absorbed by a mound of earth. The two acts of this play dramatise the process in which the earth seems to consume her and, simultaneously, documents her increasing inability to sustain an image of herself as her memories define that image. In *Not I* Beckett attempts to eliminate the image of character completely, presenting an illuminated mouth that speaks involuntarily, reciting the peculiar history of an old woman who cannot speak the pronoun 'I' and denies her own subjectivity.

Beckett's early plays almost invariably present characters whose death seems imminent. The words they speak sound as if they have spoken them often. In later plays speech assumes the form of a recitation the characters perform regularly, and Beckett provides suggestions that this particular recitation may be the last of a series. In the most recent plays the characters do not speak the recitation but experience that text as sounds that revolve in consciousness. The connection between character and recitation grows increasingly tenuous. Beckett's theatrical control allows him to present the basic paradigm of establishing and dissolving an image of character in concentrated and increasingly elliptical texts.

When Samuel Beckett began to work with Roger Blin on the first production of *Godot*, he had almost no experience in the practical techniques of theatrical performance. The theatrical viability of *Godot* is, probably, a product of an intuitive understanding of dramatic conventions that came from his skilful reading of a variety of important plays. Since that first production, Beckett has become increasingly involved in the British and continental productions of his plays. His dramas have been directed and performed by fine theatre artists, and he has had the opportunity to see his works exceptionally well realised. A chronological reading of his plays reveals his developing understanding of the physical resources of the theatre: the communicative power of light and its subtle changes, the significance of a character's movement in and out of a lighted space, the value of an actor's intense concentration upon a focused image, and the dynamic transitions possible in subtle modulations of a disciplined voice. The texts of Beckett's plays have become full statements of the mode of production they require, and his published texts encompass the vision of both playwright and director. The Beckett text is not a scenario for the improvisation of an inventive director or actor. The playwright describes the physical action if it is not implicit in the speech, and he prescribes the rhythm in the careful placement of the recurring pauses that mark his plays. Beckett's increasing involvement in production led him to assume the responsibility of directing in several major revivals of his plays: *Godot, Endgame, Happy Days*, and *Krapp's Last Tape* in Germany; *Krapp's Last Tape* and *Not I* in Paris; and *Happy Days* in London.

Beckett's work as a director reflects his concern as a playwright. He insists that actors realise the tempo and rhythm of his speeches and duplicate that kind of rhythm in movement and gesture. His productions are carefully and precisely choreographed; that is, the actor's focus, inflection, movement and gesture are worked out and set in rehearsal to be repeated in performance without spontaneous modification. He directs his attention to the colour, form and texture of scenic elements. He works carefully with designers and technicians to achieve the subtle modulations of light his plays demand, and he ensures that these transitions are played within the rhythmic structure he senses.

As Beckett's knowledge of the physical resources of the theatre has become more comprehensive and as he has become more experienced as a playwright, his plays have grown increasingly more economical in their use of both language and scenery. His proficiency in the manipulation of the physical aspects of production has not led him to use those resources more extensively but, on the contrary, to use them more sparingly – yet with an increased understanding of their power. Some people claim that Beckett's plays have grown more and more untheatrical. I believe the opposite is true: that Beckett's theatrical strategy is one of refining and distilling. He gradually eliminates everything from the text that is not absolutely required to communicate the image he desires to create. His plays become more and more theatrical in that they demonstrate his growing reliance on the intensified theatrical image in combination with an abbreviated text.

The image of a human character in space undergoing the transitions that are possible because that image is extended in time constitutes the fundamental material of theatrical performance. Beckett's radical simplification of the dramatic event allows us to see the basic conventions of representing characters in space and time with sharp clarity. The schematic simplicity of his use of these conventions has taught us, I believe, a great deal about the communicative power of the theatrical images of character, space and time. Consequently, the following chapters concentrate upon the text of each of Beckett's major plays as it operates in performance. I divide the discussion of each play into these three divisions, recognising, of course, that conventions of character, space and time are interrelated parts of a whole. The limits of consciousness form the boundaries of Beckett's sense of reality, and the spectator's imagination, not the physical stage, is the arena of Beckett's theatre. The hypothetical audience, therefore, remains a significant presence throughout my discussion of Beckett's plays.

2
'Waiting for Godot'

On 5 January 1953 *Waiting for Godot* challenged its first theatre audience with a dramatic work that seemed radically different from any they had witnessed before. The spectators at the tiny Théâtre Babylone saw a play in which two actors, representing indigent tramps named Vladimir and Estragon, perform a series of routines on a stage marked only by a mound and a single tree. Two other men, a master and his servant, pass through, stopping with them for a time. The tramps claim to be stationed at this site to meet a man they call Godot. Late in the first act a young boy arrives to deliver a message that this man has postponed their appointment until the next day. With some variation the second act repeats the events of the first. Godot never comes.

In the early history of the play many people believed that the name Godot was the key to a hidden allegory and that if this name were deciphered, the 'meaning' of the play would be clear. Some saw the letters of Godot as the diminutive of God, and others noted that the name

14

transposes the sounds of Didi and Gogo, the names the tramps use for each other. More sophisticated spectators realised that the identity of Godot was irrelevant to Beckett's dramatisation of waiting. The obscurity of Godot's relationship to the tramps contributes to the general absence of contextual detail that isolates Vladimir and Estragon in a kind of limbo, and it is precisely this absence that gave the first audiences of the play the sense that *Godot* uses the resources of the theatre in a new way.

Jean Anouilh, the leading French playwright of the forties and fifties, recognised *Godot*'s significance immediately. He claimed that the première of Beckett's play was as important an event as the first Parisian performance of Luigi Pirandello's *Six Characters in Search of an Author* thirty years before.[1] In 1923 Georges Pitoëff's production of Pirandello's play at the Comédie Champs Élysées changed the course of the French theatre, generating the exploration of illusion and reality that marks the period between the two world wars. Roger Blin's production of *Waiting for Godot* signalled as bold a change in direction. Martin Esslin characterised this theatrical revolution in an influential book that gave the movement its name, *The Theatre of the Absurd*.[2] *Godot* did not initiate this new stage in the *avant-garde*; the first plays of Ionesco and Genet precede it. Beckett's play, however, stimulated the imagination of theatre audiences more keenly than any other of the early absurdist dramas. Within a few years *Godot* had been performed all over the world, and the play became the emblem of the new movement in the theatre.

While Esslin recognised the differences among Ionesco, Genet and Beckett, he found their presentation of the basic absurdity of the human condition to be the common factor that related them to each other. He used the notion of absurdity defined by Camus in *The Myth of Sisyphus*: the idea that man is estranged from his universe because he no longer believes in any of the rational schemes that explain it. It was not their existential perspective that made the absurdists innovative. The precepts of Jean-Paul Sartre's philosophical system had influenced the theatre of the preceding decade in the plays of Albert Camus and Sartre himself; however, the existential message of these playwrights speaks within conventionally structured plays, which do not differ substantially from the plays of Anouilh and Giraudoux that dominated the theatre of the 1940s.

The plays of Ionesco, Genet and Beckett deliberately violate the conventions of realism by refusing to create images of human beings who practise plausible behaviour in familiar scenes within the co-ordinates of chronological time. Ionesco's *The Bald Soprano*, written in 1948 and produced for the first time in 1950, presents two couples speaking in apparent gibberish, using language arbitrarily, exchanging sounds without significance. One couple performs a remarkable parody of the classical recognition scene in which they discover that they must be man and wife since they share the critical coincidences of the same apartment, bedroom, bed and child. Ionesco's early plays present characters whose identity fluctuates from moment to moment, whose speech demonstrates the unreliability of language, and whose environments may shift as rapidly as their personalities. The plays of Jean Genet embody an equally problematic vision of reality, and subtly question the concepts of character and language.

Absurdist drama shares in the rejection of realism that began at the end of the nineteenth century and directed the experiments of symbolism, expressionism and surrealism. These movements claimed that realism represented merely the surface of experience, ignoring the presence of profound realities that could be evoked in freer, more subjectively organised forms. In their emphasis upon the dynamic processes of the unconscious mind, symbolism, expressionism and surrealism questioned the significance of objective reality. The major plays of the Theatre of the Absurd question the integrity of both objective and subjective visions of experience. Ionesco's people are not victimised human beings trapped within the superficiality of their society. They are nothing more than the superficial roles they assume; they perceive nothing more than the banality of their language reveals. Genet's oppressed servants in *The Maids* are not potentially creative beings who have been warped by their social structure; their psyches are the images they see reflected in their mistress's eyes, just as her dominant identity is created by their ambivalent servility. The lack of detailed information about Vladimir and Estragon does not suggest a rich inner life that Beckett refuses to objectify. These characters are no more psychologically complex than they appear to be. Vladimir and Estragon sustain their identities within the forms of behaviour that habit has imposed upon them. They have no other experience and perceive no other reality.

The principal structural characteristic that the absurdist plays share is their opacity. Each presents obstacles that interfere with the spectator's immediate comprehension. Language, characterisation, setting and plot do not coalesce into a unified representation of human behaviour; and audiences cannot easily assimilate the fragmented, disjunctive and contradictory images the play puts forward. The spectator may, of course, attend superficially to the apparently alogical sequence of images and enjoy the performance as an exercise in theatricality.

Yet these plays call for a detailed consideration of the subtle and intricate relationship of their visual and textual images. Beckett's plays in particular demand the imagination and close attention required to read a difficult work of prose fiction. That is, these plays provide the spectator with an experience in the theatre that is analogous to reading Sterne's convoluted comic novel, *Tristram Shandy*, the linguistically playful text of Joyce's *Finnegan's Wake*, or the subjectively organised exploration of memory in Proust's *Remembrance of Things Past*. These novels satisfy their readers by leading them through a labyrinth of images, impressions and startling juxtapositions of ideas. The major texts of the Theatre of the Absurd pose difficulties for their audiences and set up complex problems in interpretation which demand that the spectators engage themselves with the play actively. It is important to remember that the term Theatre of the Absurd is a convenient critical device that we use to discuss the similarities among a group of playwrights. These writers did not see themselves as part of a unified aesthetic programme when they began to write plays. The particular form of *Waiting for Godot* developed as Beckett translated the kind of writing he practised in fiction into the conventions of drama.

Godot is Beckett's second play, his third if it is appropriate to include a parody of Corneille, *Le Kid*, which he wrote as a lecturer at Trinity in 1931. *Éleuthéria*, which directly precedes *Godot*, has never been produced and Beckett has withheld it from publication. The play, which I have read in typescript, dramatises the story of a young man who attempts to reject the bourgeois values of his family and complete a process of becoming nothing. His objective relates to Murphy's quest to lose his identity in a disciplined process of erasing himself from his own perception. The play uses a simultaneous presentation of two spaces, and it exercises a Pirandellian form of theatricality as a spectator enters the action and becomes hopelessly confused. When Beckett began writing *Godot*, he established a much more tightly focused and limited frame for his dialogue.

On the surface *Godot* appears to be an extended improvised dialogue, but Beckett's sense of form subtly disciplines these conversations. The play builds upon Beckett's typical model, and we witness these two old men examining and questioning their relationship to their environment. Their perception, of course, is clouded and uncertain. The unbridgeable gap between their consciousness and the scene they inhabit may well be the most powerful theatrical image in this play.

Scene

When he uses the interaction of character and scene to reveal individualising details about these old men, Samuel Beckett exploits a fundamental convention of dramatic writing. A character's perception of the space he or she inhabits often exposes a range of classifying details, marking economic status, social attitude and psychology. The response of Ibsen's Hedda Gabler to the drawing room of the villa to which her new husband has brought her, for example, clarifies her sense of confinement in the bourgeois world her marriage circumscribes. In *Hamlet* the decadence of Denmark in Claudius' reign forms the principal aspect of Shakespeare's scene, and Hamlet's perception of that corruption isolates him from the other characters, establishing the uniqueness of his perspective and the individuality of his suffering.

The presentation of the hero's relationship to the scene

of the drama functions as a basic unit of communication in performance. Consider, for example, the dynamic interaction of hero and site in Sophocles' *Oedipus Tyrannus*. When the drama begins Oedipus perceives Thebes as a place of safety, a site in which he is free from the threat of the abhorrent deeds predicted by the oracles. In the course of his learning he discovers that Thebes has been, indeed, the scene of greatest danger, the place where he committed parricide and incest.

In both the classical drama and the drama of Elizabethan England, plays were performed in architectural spaces that were almost neutral in value. The language of the plays established both the literal and the imaginative quality of the scene. The façade of the *skene* in the Greek theatre and the tiring-house of the Elizabethan playhouse provided a practical structure for entrances, exits and tableaux and an emblematic image that could suggest a palace or public structure when required. In the eighteenth and nineteenth centuries, however, theatrical scenery became complex and flexible. Stage pictures contained specific references that established connections in the spectator's mind, and visual images rather than the text spoken by the characters became the primary means of defining place in the theatre. The precisely written scenic descriptions of the texts of Ibsen and Chekhov contain specific details that function as reference points, relating the stage picture to a particular socio-economic world. Even though the scenic image itself has strong communicative value, the dramatic realists of the late nineteenth century exploited the interaction of character and scene, using the character's perception of the space and the objects it contains to reveal an individual psychology. The garret in *The Wild Duck* functions as an image of adaptation, accommodation and regressive shelter for those who retreat into it; the physical presence of the cherry orchard in Chekhov's final play encompasses the Ranevskys' vision of themselves and marks the fragility of their condition.

Beckett's innovation consists in the radical revision of the number of images his figures have at their disposal to characterise themselves. Beckett graphically describes the places his characters inhabit. None of his details of scene or light is extraneous, but those details mark the absence rather than the presence of the signs of nature and culture. The undifferentiated landscape of *Godot* holds no detail that would give Vladimir or Estragon a personal connection to the location. The single tree allows them to improvise upon the idea of hanging, but they soon exhaust the conceptual or conversational possibilities of that object. The figure of the tree is sufficiently neutral to justify Estragon's doubt that the site of Act Two is identical to the scene of Act One. The combination of their failing memory and bare environment forces these two characters to focus upon their basic human processes, and the critical elements of their experience become their ill-fitting shoes and hats, their problems with urination and defecation, their inadequate food, and – most significantly – their relationship with each other.

In the fiction that precedes *Godot* Beckett uses the voice of a single protagonist who, in isolation, explores his own consciousness. These narrators have no companion at the moment of composition. They write in empty rooms as bleak as the landscape of *Godot*, but – in memory or invention – they create graphically rich descriptions of place. The theatrical image of a couple interacting with each other in a neutral space constitutes a departure from the structure of the novels. Colin Duckworth claims that Beckett turned to writing *Godot* because he was dissatisfied with the prose of his novels, and John Fletcher notes that Beckett described his work on the play as an escape from the 'wildness and ruthlessness' of the novels.[3] The strict limitations of the dramatic form clearly challenged Beckett to produce a different kind of prose.

The text of Molloy's writing, which an unidentified man collects periodically, consists of a detailed, though enigmatic, record of his memory as he reconstructs his journeys to his mother's room. He starts out on a bicycle but is later forced to walk and then crawl as his legs fail him. He is found and taken to the room he now occupies. *Malone Dies* repeats the situation of a man confined to a room writing pages that are collected by some unidentified figure. The writing in both novels is rich in physical detail. Molloy, for example, pictures himself travelling through a landscape that he describes graphically:

> . . . the principal beauty of this region was a kind of strangled creek which the slow grey tides emptied and filled, emptied and filled. And the people came flocking from the town, unromantic people, to admire this spectacle. Some said, There is nothing more beautiful than these wet sands. Others, High tide is the best time to see the creek of Ballyba. How lovely then that leaden water, you would swear it was stagnant, if you did not know it was not. And yet others held it was like an underground lake.[4]

The landscape that Molloy 'recollects' here is subtly demonic, but the specific images are grounded in Beckett's memory of the Irish setting in which he places Molloy's quest.

While in *Molloy* the landscape is the created image of its hero's consciousness, in *Godot* the objectivity of the dramatic form demands that the space which the spectator sees and the characters who inhabit it be separate. This division allows the audience to observe the processes in which Vladimir and Estragon perceive and mediate the details of the scene. We see the scene and, as well, witness the ways in which the consciousness of each character uses the details of that space to establish a sense of his relationship to external reality.

Vladimir and Estragon respond to the scene differently. Vladimir perceives it in terms of its difference from the Macon country although he struggles for the memory of the site of their earlier experience:

VLADIMIR: All the same, you can't tell me that this (*gesture*) bears any resemblance to . . . (*he hesitates*) . . . to the Macon country for example. You can't deny there's a big difference.

ESTRAGON: The Macon country! Who's talking to you about the Macon country?

VLADIMIR: But you were there yourself, in the Macon country.

ESTRAGON: No I was never in the Macon country! I've puked my puke of a life away here, I tell you! Here! In the Cackon country![5]

This passage illustrates a rhetorical scheme that Beckett uses again and again in *Godot*. Vladimir prods Estragon into admitting that he remembers some fact. Vladimir seems motivated to do this by his desire to locate events in space and time and also by his desire to pass the time in their game of interrogation and response. Estragon is not concerned with the identification of events in a temporal or spatial framework. His present experience defines his life at the moment and represents, in its essence, what his experience has always been. Estragon refuses to invest the difference between the Macon country and the Cackon country with significance, denying the validity of Vladimir's judgement. He then shifts into the statement of an abstract concept: his recognition that the immediate moment and the immediate place constitute a concentrated image of what life is for him. He sees this barren landscape as a muckheap, *the* muckheap in which he has spent his life. Vladimir's attempt to individualise it infuriates him. Beckett is not suggesting that the tramps did not travel from the Macon country to the Cackon; he suggests that the difference between the two sites is significant to Didi and not to Gogo.

In *The Unnamable*, the final novel of the trilogy that Beckett completed after *Godot*, he combines the antithetical perceptions of the couple into the shifting vision of a single consciousness. Mahood is the strange hero of this novel, a limbless torso confined in a jar that hangs before a restaurant. He proceeds through a troubled discourse in which he describes his relationship to the space he inhabits:

> I hope this preamble will soon come to an end and the statement begin that will dispose of me. Unfortunately I am afraid, as always, of going on. For to go on means going from here, means finding me, losing me, vanishing and beginning again, a stranger first, then little by little the same as always, in another place, where I shall say I have always been. . . .[6]

The *persona* who says these words recognises that to speak the discourse is to move toward the end of the text: silence and death. The discourse itself consists of a succession of the discoveries and losses of the self as the object of the narrative and a repetition of the experience of finding the space one inhabits to be strange and then identifying it as familiar. This combination of familiarity and strangeness characterises the relationship between self and environment that Beckett uses throughout his writing. The site of *Waiting for Godot*, the Cackon country as Vladimir identifies it, may be alien to this couple, an unfamiliar place. However, as Estragon perceives it, the bareness and hostility of this place is typical and, hence, familiar. Each of Beckett's characters recognises that no evidence which he perceives is verifiable; no object, no place, no voice, no statement spoken or heard is unequivocally certain.

As Mahood's existence has no reality apart from the discourse he speaks, this particular section of the Cackon country has no identity apart from the tramp's verbal invention.

Time

In the novels Beckett represents an individual consciousness in the immediate act of composition, self-consciously detailing his present experience, inventorying his possessions and articulating certain unverifiable images of the past. The writer–hero does not focus precisely on the past as past *per se*; his attention remains on the process of writing, assimilating the images of the past as they voice themselves in his consciousness at present. Molloy states: 'Yes, I work now, a little like I used to, except that I don't know how to work any more. That doesn't matter apparently. What I'd like now is to speak of the things that are left, say my goodbyes, finish dying.'[7]

The infinitive phrase 'to speak of the things that are left' describes the action of each of these narrators. The act of speaking/writing constitutes their being, and 'the things that are left' – both the physical objects in their immediate possession and the images of the past that inhabit their minds – form the material of their discourses. In Beckett's terms, the retrospective act is a mode of thought, perhaps *the* mode of thought, but the past has presence only in the discourse that the character speaks. Speaking that narrative postpones the ultimate silence of death. Mahood confronts that realisation directly:

> . . . all these questions I ask myself. It is not in a spirit of curiosity. I cannot be silent. About myself I need know nothing. Here all is clear. No, all is not clear. But the discourse must go on. So one invents obscurities. Rhetoric.[8]

Creating a discourse provides Beckett's heroes with the illusion of self-analysis, but that analysis remains illusory because consciousness cannot verify the material it considers. These narrators recognise the epistemological problem – the uncertainty of their knowledge. While they realise that their discourse manifests not their knowledge but their invention, they also recognise that sustaining the discourse keeps the silence at bay. However, the need to keep repeating the words of that text reduces it to a formal exercise that has no core of meaning apart from its utility in creating a sense of time. The habitual repetition of their story has destroyed the power of these words to signify, distancing them from two earlier moments: the time of the original event that the words attempt to describe and the time at which these words were originally put into a composition. Consequently, the words themselves constitute part of 'the things that are left', the residue but not the authentic object of the creative act.[9] In that sense,

Beckett's characters do not confront the past; they confront the words in which they may at one time, perhaps, have perceived the past. They cannot bridge the distance between these words and the events, objects or persons the text attempts to signify. These people can never be certain, therefore, that the original event that the words attempt to invoke actually took place.

Beckett's Malone spends his final days telling stories to himself. 'I shall soon be quite dead at last in spite of all. . . . While waiting I shall tell myself stories if I can.'[10]

Each of these writers seeks a sense of his own *persona* as the hero of the narrative and also as the storyteller, the writer reflected in his writing. The characters of Beckett's fiction and drama also maintain another equally energetic quest: the search not for selfhood but for selflessness, silence. They seek their identity through discourse; they attempt to perceive the *persona* signified by the pronoun 'I'. As Mahood says in *The Unnamable*: '. . . you must say words, as long as there are any.' However, as the later works clarify, these words form a rigid network that imprisons the self as well as defines it.

When Beckett began writing *Waiting for Godot* in early October 1948, he temporarily laid aside the equation between past and present which he was using in the trilogy. In this play the characters do not use images of the past to create a sense of their identity within time. They either cannot or will not sustain a concept of the continuity of their experience by assimilating images of the past. Consequently, they must invent and improvise with the material they find in their present situation: the barren landscape, their own physical processes and the painful failure of these processes, the presence of Pozzo and Lucky, and the potential help to be offered by Godot. The appointment with him constitutes the only significant moment in their temporal scheme. That event would terminate their current stage of existence and mark their transition into some new but unspecified mode of being. Vladimir perceives all their activity up to that potential moment in terms of that event. However, the deeds they perform in waiting relate to that objective arbitrarily. Their physical actions and verbal exchanges do nothing to provoke or to stimulate Godot's arrival; nor does their activity prepare them in any sense. The notion of waiting, as a strategy to order their experience, gives them a general sense of purpose, but in waiting time seems suspended. The actual process of identifying their activity as waiting, however, names their immediate experience and gives them the sense that their random activity holds a coherent structure. The activity of waiting provides the form and much of the content of their *discourse.* Estragon's dependence upon Vladimir leads him to join his partner in creating a rhetoric of waiting. To give up their discussion of Godot, however limited it is, would be to give up their sense of being specifically located within space and time.

In an article comparing the trilogy and the major plays, I related the project of waiting in *Godot* to the projects of writing in the novels.[11] In the novels the three speakers repeat a familiar discourse, rehearsing images and anecdotes whose repetition has become habit. Few such words remain the possession of Vladimir and Estragon, and this freedom from the imagery of a past sets *Godot* apart from Beckett's other writing. Early in the second part of the play Vladimir and Estragon perform a stichomythic exchange that recognises their deliberate attempt to be free of the past. This particular moment in *Godot* seems puzzling and enigmatic outside the context of Beckett's earlier writing:

VLADIMIR: You're right, we're inexhaustible.
ESTRAGON: It's so we won't think.
VLADIMIR: We have that excuse.
ESTRAGON: It's so we won't hear.
VLADIMIR: We have our reasons.
ESTRAGON: All the dead voices.
VLADIMIR: They make a noise like wings.
ESTRAGON: Like leaves.
VLADIMIR: Like sand.
  (*Silence*)
ESTRAGON: Like leaves.
VLADIMIR: They all speak at once.
  (*Silence*)
ESTRAGON: Each one to itself.
VLADIMIR: Rather they whisper.
ESTRAGON: They rustle.
VLADIMIR: They murmur.
  (*Silence*)
ESTRAGON: They rustle.
VLADIMIR: What do they say?
ESTRAGON: They talk about their lives.
VLADIMIR: To have lived is not enough for them.
ESTRAGON: They have to talk about it.

As Beckett differentiates Vladimir and Estragon, the more aggressive and dominant Didi attempts to locate events specifically within space and time, and Gogo resists that practice of perceiving their experience. In this sequence of dialogue Estragon expresses the motive of his resistance, clarifying his desire to lose himself in immediate activity. He consciously attempts to separate himself from the past or, to be more specific, to avoid those images of the past that come to his consciousness as *dead voices*.

This exchange also illustrates once again Beckett's

29

technique in building a scene between these two characters. The image of the *dead voices* provides them with an opportunity to improvise upon the idea of the sound of the voices, extending their conversation by listing similes. When they return to the thought itself, to discuss the content of the voices, Vladimir cries, 'Say something!', but Estragon is incapable of speech. In crisis, Vladimir proposes that they 'Wait for Godot.' Vladimir assigns Godot a function that is, in Mahood's terms, an invented obscurity. The energy these two expend in waiting equates with the effort Molloy and Malone make to sustain their discourse, and yet the texts that the heroes of the novels rehearse do not have a direct verbal counterpart in *Godot*. The equivalent is the rhetoric of the relationship of Vladimir and Estragon. The principal collection of 'the things that are left' in *Godot* consists of the habits of their partnership. Rather than perceiving the history of a profound and difficult relationship, we see its fragments and debris. The source of the individual tropes with which Didi and Gogo play out their games of dominance and submission have been lost long before the action begins. As Molloy and Malone are both sustained and trapped within their texts, these two dramatic characters are realised and compressed within the habitual routines of their relationship.

Early in the play Vladimir cites one of the two extended memories of the past that inform *Godot*:

> . . . what's the good of losing heart now, that's what I say. We should have thought of it a million years ago, in the nineties.

. . .

Hand in hand from the top of the Eiffel Tower, among

the first. We were respectable in those days. Now it's too late. They wouldn't even let us up.

Vladimir's memory of this moment in Paris 'a million years ago, in the nineties' provides a reference point, indicating that the couple have been together for approximately fifty years. This period of time defines the limit of a potential history that the characters would reveal in a conventional sequence of exposition.

In a conventionally realistic play the playwright builds an image of human character by establishing a clear relationship between the immediate behaviour of the character, which the spectator witnesses, and a series of details about the character's past released gradually in the progress of the dialogue. The spectators maintain a double focus; they develop an image of the character within the immediate moment and a sense of the character as a figure in the past. The juxtaposition of these two figures stimulates the audience to conceptualise an image of growth or development, imagining a process that bridges the past and the present *personae* of the character.

In *Waiting for Godot* Beckett sets up a temporal structure in Vladimir's early memory, but these basic co-ordinates of the fifty-year relationship are not, as in an Ibsen text, filled in with clarifying details during the progress of the play. On the contrary, the framework that Beckett sets up actually reveals the limits of what is not exposed in the continuing dialogue. This structure defines the boundaries of our ignorance. The reference to the length of their relationship stimulates us to expect the exposition of information that would explain their present situation. Beckett frustrates that expectation, and that frustration makes the audience alert to each signifying detail of their immediate behaviour, their complex pattern of dominance and submission, complicity and independence. The history that has brought them to this place is equivocal, unverifiable and – in terms of the immediate crisis – irrelevant. As the spectator responds to this challenging play, the tension between the absence of a collaborative narrative and the equally clear evidence of an extended relationship remains unresolved.

At the close of the first act, Beckett provides Estragon with a poignant memory of the past, the second extended recollection. Here he recalls an incident in which Vladimir saved him from drowning after a possible attempt at suicide. Vladimir's memory that they have been together for fifty years may stimulate Estragon's atypical reference to the past. In any case, Beckett opens and closes the act by establishing the limits of a narrative that remains undisclosed.

The history of Pozzo and Lucky, the rich landowner and his lunatic slave who have been together for sixty years, constitutes a kind of sub-plot, offering a variation on the basic couple. Their physical image – the dominating Pozzo marked with the accoutrements of wealth and the subservient Lucky, drooling and burned with the rope that confines him – suggests a rich and detailed history that has brought them to this place and time. However, only a few details of that narrative come to the surface. Pozzo reveals that Lucky has functioned as a kind of tutor–entertainer over the years he has been in his service; but the rich resources of his mind have deteriorated into a single verbal presentation. This apparently meaningless verbal performance begins:

Given the existence as uttered forth in the public works of Puncher and Wattmann of a personal God quaquaquaqua with white beard quaquaquaqua outside time without extension who from the heights of divine apathia divine athambia divine aphasia loves us dearly with some exceptions for reasons unknown but time will tell and suffers like the divine Miranda . . . .

As Anselm Atkins analyses this jumbled and repetitious speech, the message of God's withdrawal from human concern, the petrefaction of the cosmos, and the insignificance of human existence form the basic subjects.[12] The speech provides Beckett's clearest image in *Waiting for Godot* of rhetoric reduced to habit. These words, apparently once invested with resonant significance, constitute the residue of an intellect; all that remains is the suggestion of significance, buried in a meaningless repetition of cant phrases. As with Vladimir and Estragon, we see the remains but not the substance of their life together. The firmly entrenched personal conventions of interaction they exhibit reveal the fact that their relationship exists only as habit.

The second act of *Waiting for Godot* puts the same two couples together in an analogous encounter. Beckett boldly undercuts the narrative expectations of his audience by presenting the second act as a formal repetition of the structure of the first. Vladimir introduces this act by singing a round. The temporal sequence of a round offers the potential of infinite repetition, and the connection between the original event the song describes and its repetition grows progressively distant and tenuous. The implication is clear: as Vladimir and Estragon resume their process of waiting one more time, the connection between that process itself and their original intention weakens. The habit of waiting resolves into a pattern that circumscribes their experience.

Repetition operates in *Godot* as a unifying principle of

organisation; repetition replaces the kind of plotting that spectators perceive as development or transition. The second act is shorter, but in each of the two divisions of the play the old men meet at twilight to wait for Godot, exchange observations and engage in a series of verbal and non-verbal routines to pass the time, encounter Pozzo and Lucky who travel through the scene, and receive an identical message from Godot delivered by a young boy. Several sequences of dialogue and stage business in the second act repeat the material of the first. Each act, as well, ends with the following exchange:

ESTRAGON: Well, shall we go?
VLADIMIR: Yes, let's go.

Both these pairs of lines is qualified by the stage direction: *'They do not move.'*

Vladimir's dialogue with the young emissary from Godot forms another repetition. In both acts the old man's interrogation of the boy includes the question, 'It wasn't you came yesterday?' and the child's denial. This question, of course, suggests that the day represented in the first act is not the first in the potential series of days in which Vladimir and Estragon wait for Godot. The repetition of the structure of Act One in Act Two holds open the possibility that similar days will pass in which the two will meet at twilight to wait for Godot and be visited by a young boy who will offer the same message. The audience would have every reason to expect a third repetition if the play were not identified formally as 'a tragicomedy in two acts'. Beckett undermines the spectator's assumption that the event he dramatises is unique, the presentation of an action that occurs once in time such as Oedipus' discovery of his identity, Hamlet's struggle with the notion of revenge, and Lear's abdication. *Godot* presents each act as a metonym of a serial succession of days.

Beckett refuses to clarify whether or not the break between the acts represents the passing of a single night. The addition of leaves to the single tree marks some change, but the transformation of Pozzo and Lucky constitutes the principal difference between the two acts. In Act Two Lucky remains burdened with luggage and connected to Pozzo with a rope; but now he is mute and his master blind. Vladimir questions Pozzo:

> VLADIMIR: We met yesterday. (*Silence*) Do you not remember?
> POZZO: I don't remember having met anyone yesterday. But to-morrow I won't remember having met anyone to-day. So don't count on me to enlighten you.
>
> · · ·
>
> POZZO: (*suddenly furious*) Have you not done tormenting me with your accursed time! It's abominable! When! When! One day, is that enough for you, one day he went dumb, one day I went blind, one day we'll go deaf, one day we were born, one day we shall die, the same day, the same second, is that not enough for you? (*calmer*) They give birth astride of a grave, the light gleams an instant, then it's night once more. (*He jerks the rope*) On!

In Pozzo's opinion, to differentiate one moment from the next is an arbitrary and pointless exercise. His notion of undifferentiated time relates to Estragon's perception of the insignificance of the difference between the Cackon country and the Macon country. In his blindness Pozzo has lost his sense of personal history and the correlated notions of time and sequence.

35

The structural sequence of the two acts, the second repeating the first, represents time as a collection of units that add up to the larger whole of a week, a month, a year or a lifetime. Here time does not build a history or even a continuous narrative. In *Waiting for Godot* the characters do not perceive the succession of days they experience as a progression through time or as the collection of units that add up to a larger whole. Day succeeds day, but the connection between two particular days remains arbitrary. Beckett gives us no real assurance that the days represented are continuous, the second coming immediately after the first. Vladimir expends a certain energy in attempting to make the connection, but Estragon rejects his efforts as sophistic. Vladimir attempts to locate his experience with Pozzo and Lucky in some scheme that relates the two encounters, but Pozzo rejects that process, refusing to make an equation between yesterday and today. Estragon sleeps through his companion's critical exchange with Pozzo, and when Vladimir wakes him, he claims that his friend has dreamt the encounter. At this point Vladimir questions the validity of his perception and his ability to sustain the memory of his meeting with Pozzo and Lucky:

Was I sleeping, while the others suffered? Am I sleeping now? To-morrow, when I wake, or think I do, what shall I say of today? That with Estragon my friend, at this place, until the fall of night, I waited for Godot? That Pozzo passed, with his carrier, and that he spoke to us? Probably. But in all that what truth will there be?

Vladimir recognises that his memory of the encounter will be fixed within a verbal structure. He does not, for example, talk in terms of visual images of the meeting with Pozzo. He asks: 'Tomorrow . . . what shall I *say* of today?' And he questions the relationship between that verbal report and the truth.

Vladimir looks at the sleeping Estragon and realises that their relationship will continue within the same pattern as before. Then Vladimir extrapolates upon Pozzo's image of giving birth astride a grave:

> Astride of a grave and a difficult birth. Down in the hole, lingeringly, the grave-digger puts on the forceps. We have time to grow old. The air is full of our cries. (*He listens*) But habit is a great deadener.

Pozzo condenses the complete cycle of life into a single second. Vladimir repeats the juxtaposition of birth and death, locating both at the gravesite; he extends the single moment into a more expanded sense of time: 'We have time to *grow* old.' However, once again he undercuts himself with an epistemological question. He imagines himself sleeping, like Estragon, with someone looking at him as he stares at his friend: 'At me too someone is looking, of me too someone is saying, He is sleeping, he knows nothing, let him sleep on.' Vladimir not only questions the validity of his perception of experience, but sees himself caught within some form of sleep, dreaming his life not experiencing it directly. Beckett uses the equation of dream and performance that Shakespeare asserts at the end of *A Midsummer Night's Dream*, but Beckett makes the players dreamers rather than the audience. The eye in which Vladimir senses himself caught may be the eye of the spectator who watches him as he watches Estragon.

Character

When Samuel Beckett made the radical shift from writing the first-person novels to the composition of a dramatic text, he confronted a different set of conventions, a new group of aesthetic stringencies in which he was forced to work. The text of the novels represents the voice of the protagonist, and as the reader proceeds through these works, he identifies with an enigmatic speaker, voicing the 'I' that the narrator employs, seeing the world as the protagonist's words describe it. Seeing and hearing a dramatic performance, the spectator does not voice the words of the character as the reader of a novel speaks that text silently. The audience does not see the scene only through the perception of the character. On the contrary, the spectator sees the scene as an actual space that surrounds the character, witnessing the character's perception of that site and its significance. In Act III, scene ii of *King Lear* Shakespeare reinforces the sense of tempest within Lear's disintegrating mind by placing him within a real storm. Critics have identified the physical storm as an extension of his psychic turmoil, claiming that the scene anticipates the structural features of expressionism.[13] However, Shakespeare reveals Lear's increasing madness through the character's perception of the storm, his irrational identification with it. Here the playwright clarifies that the storm on the heath is an objective fact of the physical world he represents, and the spectator accepts the reality of the tempest and observes the specific ways in which Lear uses these natural phenomena to perceive the painful chaos of his own consciousness. The spectator does not assume that the meteorological storm is a manifestation of the psychic chaos Lear experiences. The physical presence of the storm intensifies the cruelty of

Lear's alienation from his family and, most importantly, provides him with concrete images with which he can explore his condition subjectively.

In the early twentieth century dramatic expressionism attempted to dissolve the difference between the subjective consciousness of the character and the scene in which he or she is placed by making the spatial environment reflect the distortions and idiosyncracies of the character's perception. This attempt to build scenic images that project the hero's consciousness derives from the desire of several modern playwrights to deny the significance of objective reality and to emphasise the subjective reality of the individual psyche. Since the stage space in expressionistic drama can only represent an image or collection of images within the consciousness of the protagonist, the characters with whom this hero interacts become images within his psyche as well, human images transformed by the fantasy or fear of the central figure.

The plays of the German expressionists, especially those of Toller and Kaiser, revealed the overpowering presence of political realities as they were perceived by the terrorised consciousnesses of their victim heroes. These works certainly made an impact upon twentieth-century drama, but the physical presence of the actor ensures that drama remains the most rigidly mimetic of the arts. The division between actor and setting causes playwriting to resist that process of modernism in which the subjective consciousness of the character represented subsumes the physical reality of the world that surrounds him.

In the plays of Samuel Beckett, characters and scenes are inextricably related. We cannot picture Vladimir and Estragon apart from the sterile landscape of the Cackon country – not because that scene projects their consciousness but, rather, because they use that scene to sustain their consciousness. The difference in perception between Vladimir and Estragon illustrates the techniques Beckett uses to maintain the scene, neutral as it may be, discrete from the psyches of his characters. Estragon sees his environment as ever the same, different in detail but the same in barren hostility, while Vladimir identifies the scene through its difference from an earlier environment. Beckett establishes the enigmatic quality of objective reality by presenting antithetical visions of it, refusing to resolve the difference. The ultimate significance of the actual space, and the reality it represents, will always elude its characters.

The equivocation of time and place in *Waiting for Godot* removes the possibility of interpreting the characters of Vladimir and Estragon from the perspective shaped by playwrights such as Ibsen, Strindberg and Chekhov. These writers established a firm network of social, political, psychological and biological references that establish their characters at a specific place within a particular moment in history. That is, each of these playwrights refers to a complex of determinants rather than presenting the behaviour of the character as the manifestation of a single cause. Stringberg's discussion of motive in the preface to *Miss Julie*, an important document in the history of dramatic realism, emphasises the multiplicity of factors that stimulate his heroine's action:

> . . . her mother's basic instincts, her father's improper bringing-up of the girl, her own inborn nature, and her fiancé's sway over her weak and degenerate mind. Further and more immediately: the festive atmosphere of Midsummer's Eve, her father's absence, her monthly illness, her preoccupation with animals, the erotic

excitement of the dance, the long summer twilight, the highly aphrodisiac influence of flowers, and finally chance itself, which drives two people together in an out-of-the-way room, plus the boldness of the aroused man.[14]

At various points in the text of the play, Strindberg signals our understanding of these individual causal factors by referring directly or indirectly to the systems in which we understand their operation. We do not isolate a single cause for the young woman's suicidal behaviour because we recognise the interdependence of the multiple causal factors. The resulting image of the interaction of social, economic, psychological and biological systems establishes the illusion of reality in *Miss Julie*. The convention of realism exploits the notion of the complex interrelationship of these determinants.

Consider the ways in which that interplay of systems operates in another realistic play. In Ibsen's *The Master Builder* Halvard Solness gains his success as a builder by sub-dividing land inherited by his bourgeois wife. Without financial resources himself, he uses the property to advance professionally. His opportunity to use that property comes from an accidental fire that destroys the old family home and indirectly causes the deaths of their infant sons. The loss of her home, the deaths of the children and the development of the estate intersect in Fru Solness's mind to create a keenly felt resentment of her husband. These same factors compound themselves in Solness's imagination to produce the causes of his own painful guilt. Solness's exploitation of his wife encompasses subtly interconnected sexual, economic and psychological use. It would be impossible to divide and isolate economic motivation from psychological determinism in Ibsen's play. In fact, the relationship of the various systems of reference here suggests a complex of causal factors that is, ultimately, incomprehensible. However, Ibsen's reference to the socio-economic system by which we understand the image of property in *The Master Builder* does not conflict with the psychological system by which we perceive and understand the human phenomenon of guilt. We understand Solness's ambition both in terms of the motives he gains from his class and in terms of his psychological need for dominance and power. Audiences accept the interplay of determinants, assimilating the whole complex as various systems are signalled during the performance.

In *Waiting for Godot* Samuel Beckett does not, like Ibsen, present the image of a complex interlocking of systems of determinism. Instead of recognising the interrelationship of several systems of cause, the audience confronts a series of disjunctions in *Godot*. For example, we assume that the two old men are indigent, and yet the quality of their vocabulary and the nature of their speech suggest that they are men of some education. Estragon identifies himself as a poet, ironically pointing out his tattered clothes, but nothing in the spoken memories of these men explains the source of their wit or vocabulary.

The tramps' indigence and Pozzo's and Godot's wealth as landowners place Beckett's characters in a recognisable socio-economic scheme. The relationship between Pozzo and Lucky, moreover, presents an image of master and slave that seems to refer directly to Hegel's model of lordship and bondage. In this paradigm, which strongly influenced Marx, the master alienates himself from the material world by using the slave to produce goods; and while the slave has the direct satisfaction of creating material objects, they remain alien to him because they are owned by another consciousness. The master's behaviour is determined by his relationship to the slave, and the slave fulfils the role defined by the master. In Beckett's variation the slave, Lucky, produces thoughts rather than objects; he has been Pozzo's connection to the world of intellect and culture. That world, however, has escaped them both; nothing of it remains but the words of this disturbing tirade that oppresses both servant and master.

The self-consciousness of Beckett's writing manifests itself in his perception of the relationship of the text he writes to earlier texts, his own and others. He uses specific literary and theatrical conventions with the same self-consciousness, employing a subtle irony that makes the connection between the present text and its predecessor and, simultaneously, marks the difference between them. Of course Beckett represents characters who hold sufficient typicality to stimulate our identification with them, and he exposes them in moments of acute crisis. However, at the same time these theatrical pieces present themselves with irony. The performance of *Waiting for Godot*, for example, must assume the quality of theatrical play. The juxtaposition of emotion and playfulness constitutes the Beckettian mode. After establishing an emotional moment, Beckett frequently makes a character refer to his own theatricality, shifting the spectator's emotional response into an awareness that it has been stimulated or provoked by an artifice. The placement of Estragon's reference to the off-stage toilet provides a good example. The ultimate recognition, of course, that a spectator experiences as he watches *Godot* includes a realisation that while emotion may have been generated by an artifice, nothing in experience, 'for reasons unknown', is any more authentic.

The clearest image of theatricality in *Godot* is one of

character. Beckett shapes Vladimir and Estragon as conventional stage tramps, exploiting a tradition that is rich in significance as Ruby Cohn notes in her first study of Beckett:

> The opening scene – a leafless tree near which a ragged man tugs at his boots, 'giving up *again*' [Cohn's italics], establishes the comic ambiance before a word is spoken. The Chaplin costume prepares us for the exaggerated gestures of the silent comic: Estragon tugging at and taking off his boots; Vladimir doffing, donning, and seeking lice in his hat; the ape-stance of the two friends; their exercises; their difficulties with trousers; their imitation of the tree; their lapses from the dignified vertical; their hat-juggling routine. Moreover, the Chaplin garb suggests the hero as social victim, because Chaplin so consistently and comically played that role. Become a symbol, Chaplin's vulnerability seems willed by fate, underwritten in the cosmic order.[15]

The absence of details that would place Beckett's tramps in a plausible or historically specific situation often causes audiences to perceive them as charged, symbolic figures, as twentieth-century everymen. However, Beckett has not eliminated the detail that would ground *Godot* in the conventions of realism in order to write an allegory that presents his characters within a clear philosophical or theological scheme. No key exists that will unlock the enigmas of this play, and Vladimir and Estragon do not form religious archetypes. While biblical imagery does play its role in *Godot*, that imagery does not form a cohesive network of references to any clear statement. The religious images are there in the same function as the ill-fitting hats and boots, as the refuse of some earlier time, as part of the collection of 'things that are left' which these old men exploit in their desperation to find ideas, objects, words to pass the time.

Beckett's stage fools, in the tradition of Shakespeare's wise jesters, point out human folly; however, Beckett's characters here direct their mockery principally to themselves. Ruby Cohn notes Beckett's use of the traditional comic types that are set down in the *Tractatus*, a critical work which may have been written by Aristotle.[16] This text identifies the comic impostor, the *alazon* who pretends to be more than he is, and the *eiron*, the self-deprecator who mocks and often unmasks the pretentious disguise of the *alazon*. Beckett's tramps, as *eirons*, point out the foolishness of their own posturing, deflating their own tendencies to act as *alazons*. In establishing the differences between the two, Beckett gives Estragon the more ironic voice:

ESTRAGON: (*coldly*) There are times when I wonder if it wouldn't be better for us to part.
VLADIMIR: You wouldn't go far.
ESTRAGON: That would be too bad, really too bad. (*Pause*) Wouldn't it, Didi, be really too bad? (*Pause*) When you think of the beauty of the way. (*Pause*) And the goodness of the wayfarers. (*Pause. Wheedling*) Wouldn't it, Didi?

Estragon undercuts Vladimir's attempt to belittle his independence, recognising the bullying pretence of Didi's dominance. But his bitter perception of the hostility of the world that he would confront on his own deflates his own false independence.

The ironic quality of Beckett's tramps would make them appropriate figures in a conventional pastoral drama,

45

commenting on the nature of society from the perspective of those outside it. In fact, Beckett's use of the pastoral landscape in *Godot* does, I think, make a self-conscious reference to the literary and theatrical mode of pastoral. The pastoral or satyric scene, a glade bound by the forest, was one of the three conventionalised settings of the Italian Renaissance. The structure of pastoral comedy, best known in Shakespeare's versions, usually employs the country landscape as a place of retreat, an escape for the urban or courtly characters who use it for a temporary exile. Here sophisticated figures from the upper class mix freely with people of a lower station in life, often gaining in wisdom from that association. As Sir William Empson notes, the mixture of classes forms an important aspect of the genre.[17] Beckett's *Godot* clearly establishes the difference in class among those who come into its rural landscape; the reference to genre, however, remains ironic. We have no sense that the interaction between classes has been purposeful, and we have no hope that the tramps' exile in the Cackon country will prepare them to re-enter their ordinary world with increased wisdom and understanding. Indeed, there seems to be no other world, and Beckett's Cackon country is neither Arden nor Illyria.

While Vladimir and Estragon are not 'realistic' characters, spectators identify with them as they attempt to obtain some grasp on their sense of being and their individuality. At the same time sophisticated audiences recognise that as Beckett uses them he plays with traditional comic devices, exploiting them as images of theatricality. This kind of disjunction serves to disorient the spectators, puzzling them and putting them on guard. This disorientation is compounded by the interpretative puzzles the play presents.

At critical points the spectator's imagination seeks a key

to the play's complexity, attempting to translate the experience represented into some comprehensible intellectual argument. The biblical allusions suggest the possibility of a religious interpretation; the obvious connections to pastoral drama open the possibilities for literary and theatrical analysis; the references to specific economic and social differences among the characters suggest the potential for a socio-economic or Marxian explanation of the puzzles the performance projects. None of these, however, serves as an adequate system for incorporating all of its parts, even though each argument is provoked at some point. Using any single ideological system to interpret *Waiting for Godot* would be a misreading of Beckett's play. Any performance that attempted to clarify one of these interpretations of the action without giving equal emphasis to the other possibilities would reduce the experience of the spectator. Beckett exhibits and examines the nature of consciousness and the forms in which characters perceive their relationship to that which is external to the self. His representations of character are neither realistic nor allegorical. That is, he reveals no more of the specific historical context in which he places his figures than they themselves recognise. His characterisations are not abstract since these people deal with specific places, times and objects. They focus upon the minutiae of experience because no larger framework has validity for them. The differing elements of their experience do not cohere so that they cannot formulate a larger structure which would make their lives comprehensible to them. In Beckett's use of language and theatrical image each assignment of signification is the implementation of a fiction. That fiction is not the distortion or revision of some truth; the fictional structure is all that can be known.

The spectator's inability to order the various elements of this theatrical experience within a coherent and systematic interpretation that aligns with some existing intellectual system forces him to deal with the immediate experience as an image of reality on its own terms. The radical reduction of context in *Waiting for Godot* focuses the attention of the spectator on the following human problems: the failure of critical bodily processes, painful and difficult urination and defecation; the perception of the body as a familiar but undependable machine; the experience of being unable to identify the site in which one exists with a personal memory or sense of connection, seeing the self as an alien object in the space it inhabits; the experience of being unable to locate oneself within a coherent and comprehensible chronology, realising that any sense of the past may be, in itself, a fiction; the experience of a complex disorientation that comes from recognising that any activity engaged in must be supplied by one's own invention; the recognition of one's dependency upon another human being and the simultaneous realisation that this dependence is a trap that binds the self in habitual patterns of behaviour from which it is impossible to grow free.

The uncertainty of Godot, the obscurity of his identity and the deferral of his arrival, constitutes his significance within this drama. Godot will never come, nor will he be identified, because Beckett refuses to close the narrative with that event: the meeting remains a potentiality. The significance of Godot does not derive from the value of the figure as a specific symbol, a metaphor for authority, state or God. The value of the image derives from its use by Vladimir and Estragon as a hypothesis on which they base their behaviour. Beckett establishes a critical absence, not on the stage physically but within the cognitive processes of the two principal characters. Didi and Gogo base their action on the potentiality of the encounter with Godot, but the specific historical placement of that meeting and the actual identity of that figure remain unclear in their consciousness. They must struggle, therefore, with the problems which stem from that failure of memory, perception and knowledge. Beckett dramatises that struggle, and the processes of their grappling with that problem constitute the action of *Waiting for Godot*. At the end of the performance of this play, we sense that the future holds a series of days that will repeat themselves in patterns similar to the two we have experienced. Vladimir and Estragon are, however, old men who suffer the failure and weaknesses of age, and the succession of days cannot extend infinitely. The processes of waiting are themselves finite.

3
'Endgame'

The première production of *Endgame*, in its original French version as *Fin de partie*, took place in London at the Royal Court Theatre in April 1957 with Roger Blin and Jean Martin, *Godot*'s Pozzo and Lucky, playing Hamm and Clov. Despite the success of *Godot*, Blin had been unable to locate a theatre in Paris willing to risk a production of Beckett's new play.[1] That local inhospitality explains the peculiar event of a play in French being given its initial production in an English-speaking theatre in London. At the end of the month, however, the production moved into the small Studio des Champs Élysées. Les Editions de Minuit published the text shortly before its first production, as they did with *Godot*.[2] Beckett's translation, *Endgame*, was published in 1958, and the first production of the English text took place under Alan Schneider's direction at the Cherry Lane Theatre in New York on 28 January 1958.[3] In October the play returned to the Royal Court in its English translation, this time directed by George Devine who, like Blin, also played Hamm.

'Endgame'

In *Godot* Beckett explores the partnership of the two primary characters, representing the subtle complicities, compromises and patterns of acceptance and rejection that mark extended relationship. He continues that investigation in *Endgame*. The casting of Blin and Martin as Hamm and Clov suggests that Beckett may have been stimulated by their performance in *Godot* to explore the possibilities of a play that deals primarily with a master and servant. A manuscript, which may have been written as early as 1954, contains a blind and paralysed master, X, who sits in a wheelchair, and a servant, F (for factotum), who escapes to his kitchen.[4] The succeeding *Endgame* manuscripts demonstrate that Beckett's work on this play was slow and painstaking in comparison to his relatively rapid completion of *Godot*.

In the earlier drafts of the play the couple's role-playing is bolder and more self-conscious than in the final version. In the two-act form that precedes *Endgame*, Clov's prototype, then identified as 'B', assumes other personalities in his games with his master. In the first act he dresses as a woman, disguised in a blonde wig, false breasts and a skirt. At the end of the second act he plays the role of a young boy. In the final version of the play Beckett replaced the bold dynamics of role-playing with the subtle adjustments that Clov makes in his behaviour in order to respond to the particular mood that Hamm adopts. While Clov always seems to maintain an ironic distance from Hamm's rhetorical declamations, he knows the words to speak to assist his master in sustaining the routines the blind man plays. However, these nuances of role-playing complicate the spectator's response to the characters because it is difficult to determine if specific references in their dialogue relate to their basic relationship or to the structure of the games they share.

51

The play begins with Clov's comic routine with the room's high windows and his ladder. Then the infirm servant uncovers the seated figure of the blind and paralysed master and announces: 'Finished, it's finished, nearly finished, it must be nearly finished.' In the course of the play the master displays his tyranny over the servant and his parents, legless torsos confined in ash bins. At the end of the play the servant stands ready to depart. Has the relationship between him and his master reached its final moment; will he depart and leave his master to die?

Endgame seems to imitate that simple action. As Hamm and Clov consider the events of this day, Clov states that 'Something is taking its course.' That 'course' may be the unique movement in time that proceeds towards the dissolution of their relationship: Clov's departure and Hamm's death. However, Beckett also establishes the possibility that Clov's preparation for departure and Hamm's movement into solitude and silence are not elements of a uniquely authentic event but simply a routine that the two men perform. The text offers both possibilities:

> Finished, it's finished, nearly finished, it must be nearly finished. (*Pause*) Grain upon grain, one by one, and one day, suddenly, there's a heap, a little heap, the impossible heap. (*Pause*) I cannot be punished any more.

The pronoun of Clov's statement 'it's finished . . .' has no specific referent in either the French or the English text. This openness of reference is typical of Beckett's use of language. 'It' may signify Clov's life or, in a more qualified reference, 'it' may signify Clov's life with Hamm.

Beckett follows Clov's sequence of 'finished' with the image of the impossible heap of grains. This image reduces Clov's sense of process – the completed movement of 'it's finished' – to a meaningless succession of incidents, the accumulation of units that eventually forms a heap. Even though the pile of grains is completed, it cannot be interpreted, it remains an inchoate mass; and that perception robs the potential satisfaction Clov may find in seeing life as a totality, a 'finished' product. In other words, Clov's reference to Zeno's paradox exercises the notion that while any object of magnitude is subject to division, the act of perceiving it as separated components identifies that object, not as a discrete entity, but, rather, as a collection of individual segments. In that sense, Clov's assertion that whatever is happening is coming to an end and therefore constitutes a whole is balanced by his perception of life as a meaningless collection of units, 'the impossible heap'.

Later in the performance we hear Hamm express the same ideas, apparently within set speeches that he recites regularly. Clov admits at one point that he speaks the words that Hamm has taught him. Language in *Endgame*, as in the trilogy and *Godot*, represents a residue, a remnant of some earlier time. Hamm's first speech comes in the form of a soliloquy that appears to be the text of a play-within-a-play. Beckett implies that he performs this text regularly. Hamm also recites his story daily; at least Clov identifies this history as 'The one you've been telling yourself all your days.' As Hamm begins his recitation, we hear the words with which Clov opened the text of *Endgame*:

Where was I?
(*Pause. Gloomily*)

It's finished, we're finished.
(*Pause*)
Nearly finished.
(*Pause*)
There'll be no more speech.

At this point the spectator may speculate that the story Hamm has been telling himself all his days may be a description of his own life. His version of the 'finished' sequence begins with the indefinite referent 'it' and then shifts into the specific '. . . we're finished. (*Pause*) Nearly finished.'[5] When the audience hears the echo of the opening lines, they may recognise that Clov was not speaking an original thought but, rather, was voicing a refrain that he has heard Hamm speak repeatedly. Clov also seems to have taken the metaphor of the grains from one of Hamm's recitations. We hear that image in the second enactment of Hamm's play-within-a-play:

> Moment upon moment, pattering down, like the millet grains of . . . (*he hesitates*) . . . that old Greek, and all life long you wait for that to mount up to a life.

The obvious speculation that Clov parrots Hamm argues against the interpretation that Clov's declaration 'it's finished' announces his perception of a unique moment in time. However, because Beckett postpones giving his audience the information that Clov's words may be mindless echoes until this point, he stimulates them to review their memory of the opening moment and adjust their response.

Clov's words and Hamm's recitation echo Christ's final words on the cross as the Gospel of St John records them: '. . . he said, It is finished: and he bowed his head and gave up the ghost' (John 19:30). If the members of the audience make the connection between the opening line and the words that immediately precede the death of Jesus, they will expect that the action of *Endgame* will end in a death. However, the spectator's perception of that first line is also qualified by an awareness of the title of the play, *Endgame, Fin de partie*, not the moment of closure in the game of chess but, rather, the final phase of play. The game of *Endgame*, of course, is not a literal reference. The spectator opens up the term to use it metaphorically as a scheme with which to interpret the action. Whereas at this early point in the performance the significance of game, as an idea or an image, has only speculative value, the question does alert us to watch the performance carefully in an attempt to determine if *Endgame* imitates the act of dying or whether it imitates a game in which the players pretend to move towards death.

Character

Beckett places Hamm and Clov in a bare but familiar room, and the roles demanded by their relationship determine their use of that space. Hamm commands and dominates the site; Clov serves him and sees the room as a prison. In that sense the characterised image of master and slave subsumes the image of space.

HAMM: What have you done with your bicycle?

CLOV: I never had a bicycle.

HAMM: The thing is impossible.

CLOV: When there were still bicycles I wept to have one. I crawled at your feet. You told me to go to hell. Now there are none.

HAMM: And your rounds? When you inspected my paupers. Always on foot?

These unelaborated references suggest that their relationship holds a variety of socio-political and psychological dimensions. The notion of rounds and paupers indicates an extensive ownership of property, and the denial of Clov's bicycle points towards a capricious bestowal and refusal of favours – the kind of arbitrary benevolence and cruelty that engenders acute resentment as well as obligation in its victims.

Beckett complicates the basic image of Hamm and Clov as master and servant with suggestions that their relationship also functions as that of father and son. The narrative Hamm recites tells of a father who comes to Hamm as a suppliant to beg for a job in order to feed himself and his starving child. The final segment of the story focuses upon the child whom the suppliant left behind, sleeping:

> In the end he asked me would I consent to take in the child as well – if he were still alive. (*Pause*) Would I consent to take in the child . . . .

Shortly before telling this story, Hamm questions Clov about his memory of the occasion when he came to Hamm's household. This exchange, typically equivocal, stimulates the spectator to speculate about the identity of Clov and the identity of his father, who is named but not described.

HAMM: Do you remember when you came here?
CLOV: No. Too small, you told me.
HAMM: Do you remember your father?
CLOV: (*wearily*) Same answer. (*Pause*) You've asked me these questions millions of times.
HAMM: I love the old questions. (*With fervour*) Ah the

56

old questions, the old answers, there's nothing like them! (*Pause*) It was I was a father to you.
CLOV: (*he looks at Hamm fixedly*) You were that to me.

. . .

HAMM: (*proudly*) But for me, (*gesture towards himself*) no father. But for Hamm, (*gesture towards his surroundings*) no home.
CLOV: (*Pause*) I'll leave you.

By setting this exchange a few pages before Hamm recites the story of the suppliant, Beckett establishes the possibility that Clov was the starving child, his actual father the suppliant, and that Hamm did, indeed, take them in his service, becoming a kind of surrogate father to the child. Hamm tells the story as an invention, but Beckett poses the possibility that it may be a history of the origin of their relationship.

These two units of the text illustrate a rhetorical pattern that Beckett uses frequently: in the first place, the relationship between the section of dialogue and the narrative Hamm recites is oblique. By placing the two units close to each other in the text Beckett gives the spectator the opportunity to make the connection, but he does not reinforce that relationship until Hamm calls for his 'son' in the final moments of the play.

Hamm's story may be interpreted as the invented fiction in which he and Clov discuss the self-created past of their experience. Beckett suggests that Clov's memory of the past is not a direct recollection but, rather, the memory of their repeated dialogues about the past: 'The old questions, the old answers'. The dialogue they speak in habitual repetition constitutes both their relationship and their history. Consequently, Beckett establishes the possibility that: (1) Hamm's story may have no connection to their relationship; (2) Hamm's story may be a history of the origin of their relationship, explaining the psychological and socio-economic limits within which they relate to each other; (3) Hamm's story may be an invention that provides the two of them with a narrative pattern in which they imagine the past and justify the present; (4) Hamm's story may be an extrapolation, embellishing and revising some actual origin that he has not revealed; (5) Hamm and Clov may not know, with any certainty, whether or not the story has a direct relationship to a past event since the point of transition between memory and invention may have been lost in a series of repetitions.

Beckett's presentation of time and his method of presenting character are closely interlocked. Each of his characters is a deteriorated and damaged figure whose image suggests a present immobility in contrast to a past vitality. Instead of witnessing the image of a person actively engaged in life, we watch the remnant of an individual whose consciousness reviews a narrative that may relate to the past, seeing himself and the objects that surround him as the residue of an earlier time. The periodic repetition of his story, however, diminishes the energy of its presentation and its ability to stimulate and enliven the mind of the storyteller. This structural model allows Beckett to represent a consciousness that is intensely focused upon the present moment and, at the same time, to create an image of extended time. Beckett conveys that sense of extension in time through carefully placed references to deterioration, consumption and loss that build the image of a slow and painful movement through the past up to this precise moment. He also establishes a sense of time by suggesting that the speeches in which

Hamm and Clov rehearse these processes are themselves old refrains that they speak again and again.

Although Hamm appears to be proceeding rather self-consciously through the experience of dying, Beckett keeps the spectators of this play uncertain as to whether Hamm is dying or imitating the action of dying. Hamm performs himself in a theatrical presentation of himself for himself. Clov, Nagg and Nell provide the necessary audience and, at times, assume the roles that Hamm's performance demands. Within Hamm's performance of himself, he aims at a series of levels of characterisation: (1) the high-mimetic and elegantly rhetorical posturing of the *persona* he plays in his play-within-a-play; (2) the ironic consciousness that deflates and interrupts this performance; (3) the *persona* that tells the stories and sees himself as a character within them; (4) the *persona* of the father played for the son (Clov); (5) the character of the son played for the parents; (6) the character of the landowner who has lost the subjects he dominated except for Clov. Each of these roles operates within its own conventions. This subtle fragmentation keeps us from responding to the image of Hamm in performance as the realistic figure of an individual psyche. While various aspects of his compound *persona* connect with our own notions of self and experience and at specific moments we identify with a particular perception that the character Hamm expresses, we do not translate the data we receive into the image of a complete psychological biography for Hamm. We can never be certain when Hamm is responding within the co-ordinates of one of his roles or whether Clov's response is conditioned by his training or the product of his own perception. Beckett's deliberate equivocation – uncertainty is the only certainty – blurs the distinction between *persona* and performance, between character and self-conscious role.

Audiences perceive the relationship of the two central figures in terms of a series of antitheses: although Hamm and Clov are bound together in various acts of complicity, each manifests a profound sense of alienation and isolation; although Hamm's authority dominates Clov, he is himself dependent upon the sight and mobility of the servant; although Hamm's authority derives from his role in the past, only the remnants of that power remain; although both Hamm and Clov perceive freedom as freedom from the constraints of their relationship, each has difficulty in moving towards the dissolution of their unequal partnership; although the subject of their habitual games is the process of ending, their attitude towards death is ambiguous, encompassing desire and fear; although they are not father and son, their relationship patterns itself on their approximation of that relationship; although the action of the play seems to move towards the end of their relationship, at the final moment of the play they remain together – providing images of potential, not actual, departure and death.

As secondary images of character, Nagg and Nell provide a simpler problem than Pozzo and Lucky. The shocking figure of old people confined in ash bins, mistreated by their son, jars the sensibility of an audience, but also creates a comic image which diffuses the pathos. Nagg's insistence on telling his story relates to Beckett's typical paradigm of consciousness and recitation. The presence of Hamm's parents, housed in containers normally holding refuse, reveals the distance between present and past in his consciousness. As human images, they function as another form of residue. Nell's possible death and Hamm's renunciation of his father participate in the movement towards silence and solitude that Hamm elects. Hamm's relentless attempt to perform his own authority creates victims, and these old people join Clov in serving the role-playing that gives Beckett's hero some sense of himself.

Beckett's subtle but persistent fragmentation of the character of Hamm demands that the audience of *Endgame* confront a wide range of possible interpretations of his behaviour. Initially spectators find it comfortable to work with one of the possible interpretations of the relationship of Hamm and Clov, organising their response within some coherent critical framework. Eventually, however, one has to give up the comfort or security of a single interpretation of *Endgame*, recognising that the play does not work towards the clarification of a meaning but, rather, towards the clarification of the impossibility of meaning. Hamm and Clov do not have a relationship determined by a history, and Beckett has not written a play that is an imitation of a relationship imagined in those terms. Hamm and Clov, or rather the actors playing Hamm and Clov, represent characters exercising certain physical gestures and patterns of language that hold an equivocal and puzzling relationship to our previous notions of drama and narrative. These actions and words hold a range of possible significance, but any significance remains potential. A single interpretation works temporarily, both for the characters and for the audience, but eventually that interpretation shifts into uncertainty. *Endgame* plays with interpretation or, rather, with various processes of provoking interpretation. Thus *Endgame* is not about character and the relationship of characters; rather the play is the theatrical embodiment of the uncertainty and equivocation implicit in the concept of selfhood and the relationship of the self to the presence of another.

Scene

In *Endgame* Beckett leaves the barren but expansive landscape of *Godot* and returns to the image of a confined room, using the kind of space in which the protagonists of the trilogy wrote their pages. The figure of Hamm, seated in a wheelchair and covered with a sheet when the performance begins, dominates the 'bare interior'. Two ash bins, which we learn later contain the legless bodies of Hamm's parents, stand downstage left; and the motionless body of Clov is stationed near the single door.

Whereas each of the two acts of *Godot* represents the same segment of the day, the transition from twilight to darkness, in *Endgame* the grey light that illuminates the room remains constant and Clov reports the increasing loss of light in the world outside of the windows. According to Hamm's and Clov's usage, one of the high windows looks out on the land and the other on the sea, echoing the division between earth and water in Genesis that constitutes a major stage in the biblical account of creation. Early in the play Clov declares that he is able to distinguish between the land and the ocean, but at the end of the play he either cannot make that distinction, or else deliberately refuses to communicate the differences he does perceive. When Hamm first asks him specific questions about the space without, Clov describes the land as 'corpsed' and the sea as 'leaden'. His second attempt to investigate the scene beyond the windows comes late in the play. Fulfilling Hamm's command, Clov makes his report, condensing his description to the single word, 'nothing', until he enlivens the moment with his report of the young boy. Beckett plays with the imagery of creation from Genesis, but he reverses the sequence. He begins with a world which divides light and darkness and separates land

and water and moves toward obscure greyness and void.[6]

In *Endgame* Beckett removes the external scene from the spectator's view. The gap between the landscape outside the windows and Hamm's consciousness cannot be bridged. Beckett gives that division a concrete, physical embodiment by removing the landscape from Hamm's vision and the vision of the audience. The objective fact of the external world has no real significance in the play, and the only landscape that can be represented is the image of the scene that Clov elects to reveal. Thus by removing the image of the external world from the spectator's perception, Beckett opens the possibility of several interpretations of Clov's descriptions of that view: (1) the world outside is in the process of change; (2) the normal fading of light in the evening makes it impossible for Clov to distinguish the difference between land-mass and ocean; (3) his failing sight clouds the difference; (4) his reports represent a perverse deception of his authoritarian master. Because each spectator shares Hamm's reliance on the accuracy of Clov's description of the scene outside the tiny windows, the audience can well understand that Hamm's dependence upon Clov's report isolates him in a peculiar uncertainty. The acutely self-conscious protagonists of the trilogy are always uncertain of the truthfulness of their own perception. Hamm suffers the additional uncertainty that the data he receives from Clov cannot be tested. Here Beckett establishes a concrete physical image of the irredeemable division between the words that identify or describe and the objects that conciousness attempts to encompass in naming them.

The writer–heroes of the trilogy recognise that language pretends to be knowledge but cannot be. They consistently correct and deny the validity of the statements they make.

Molloy claims that an original, creative use of language is impossible, because when we *create*, we merely voice the residue of lessons that were learned earlier and were then forgotten by the conscious mind.[7] In fiction, a speaker like Molloy can reverse a statement, deny the nature of an image, continually contradict and correct himself as he struggles with problems of perception. When Beckett shifts from drama to fiction, he faces the difficulty of translating that epistemological questioning into a dramatic situation. In *Godot* he solves the problem by creating a neutral space onto which Vladimir and Estragon project their opposed interpretations. The image of the outside world in *Endgame*, removed from Hamm's direct perception and present only in Clov's inadequate words, provides the unstable world that Beckett's writing demands. Beckett compounds that ambiguity in Hamm's story of the madman in the asylum.

> I once knew a madman who thought the end of the world had come. He was a painter – and engraver. I had a great fondness for him. I used to go and see him, in the asylum. I'd take him by the hand and drag him to the window. Look! There! All that rising corn! And there! Look! The sails of the herring fleet! All that loveliness! (*Pause*) He'd snatch away his hand and go back into his corner. Appalled. All he had seen was ashes. (*Pause*) He alone had been spared. (*Pause*) Forgotten. (*Pause*) It appears the case is . . . was . . . not so . . . so unusual.

Here Beckett suggests that the artist's mad solipsism causes him to see only ashes where Hamm is able to perceive the 'reality' of the fertile earth and the fruitful sea. By inserting this anecdote, the playwright poses the possibility that the landscape outside the windows of this room may be as different from Clov's report as the ashes seen by the madman are from Hamm's description. Since Clov claims that he speaks only the words that Hamm has taught him, the vision he reports may well be one that he has learned from Hamm and repeats only to satisfy him.

Like the madman, Hamm describes the outside world as 'that other Hell' and claims that 'Outside of here it's death!' Early in the play Hamm identifies the room as a shelter:

> Enough, it's time it ended, in the shelter too. (*Pause*) And yet I hesitate, I hesitate to . . . end.

'It's time it ended' echoes Clov's opening words: 'Finished, it's finished, nearly finished, it must be nearly finished.' Hamm's qualifying phrase, 'in the shelter too' suggests two locations and two times for the process of ending: a potential ending in the space of the room which the audience sees, and a possible ending that has already taken place in the world external to this room. In his original French text, *Fin de partie*, Beckett uses the noun *refuge*, a word that holds more ambiguity than shelter since it can suggest excuse or subterfuge as well as protection. Beckett originally translated *refuge* directly into English as refuge, but before publishing the English translation *Endgame*, he substituted the more precise term shelter.[8]

Close to the end of the play, Hamm returns to the image of shelter:

> There I'll be, in the old shelter, alone against the silence and . . . (*he hesitates*) . . . the stillness. If I can hold my peace, and sit quiet, it will be over with sound, and motion, all over and done with.

The image of space invoked by the noun *shelter* seems to offer Hamm some protection against the threat of silence. In Beckett's writing silence equates with death. Speaking gives the one who speaks a form of identity even if the language he invents is the text of a 'pensum one day got by heart and long forgotten'. Without language there can be no sense of identity, no self-consciousness. In *Endgame* the presence of Clov, and to a lesser degree the presence of Nagg and Nell, provides an occasion for language. Clov's function as listener, protecting Hamm from silence, makes that sterile room into a refuge, a shelter from the silence that would generate from the lack of a need to speak. In this speech, however, Hamm perceives the shelter differently; that is, he imagines himself alone within it, imagining the possibility of silence and the completion of the process that will end in his death.

Beckett does not make clear, however, that Hamm actually refers to the room that we see when he speaks of the shelter. He speaks this image in the sections he introduces by the phrase 'Me to play'. The 'shelter', therefore, may be some imaginary space in the fragmented heroic drama he performs. Molloy announces his purpose in writing his daily pages: 'What I'd like now is to speak of the things that are left, say my goodbyes, finish dying.' That intention also describes Hamm's project in *Endgame*. Beckett places Hamm and Clov in a room which contains objects that seem to stimulate memory, but their condition does not evoke the past as much as it marks the deterioration, decay and exhaustion of the present. The paucity of objects contrasts with an image of a past that held a multiplicity of objects, a time when there were bicycles, for example, or a time when Nagg and Nell rested on sawdust in their ash bins rather than sand.

Hamm's process of calling for objects and discarding

them corresponds to Molloy's desire to inventory the objects in his possession so that he can resolve his relationship to them in preparation for his death. Hamm is blind, and his perception of these objects depends, to some degree, upon Clov as a mediator. Hamm cannot verify the authenticity of any of these objects. Hamm's blindness intensifies Beckett's basic image of a consciousness struggling with the realisation that experience is a self-created fiction. Clov speaks the words that Hamm has taught him. Consequently, the presence that reflects Hamm's identity and provides him with the occasion for speech merely echoes Hamm's own words, enclosing Hamm in a self-reflexive circle.

Clov's failing but still existent sight shows that he is subject to a progressive alienation from the world external to him. The sense of that progressive blindness and immobility implies that in the past Hamm was not blind and immobile. Beckett's text allows for the possibility that when Hamm taught Clov the words that describe their world and identify the objects within it, Hamm could see that landscape. The implication here is that their relationship to the world grows increasingly uncertain and equivocal. But, in this moment – the only moment in Beckett's play that is significant to it – Hamm perceives the world primarily through the words Clov speaks to him. His connection to the outside world is diminished by Clov's failing eyesight and, quite possibly, by Clov's deteriorating memory. Hamm's prediction of his servant's eventual blindness suggests his own image of himself in space:

> One day you'll be blind, like me. You'll be sitting there, a speck in the void, in the dark, for ever, like me. Infinite emptiness will be all around you, all the resurrected dead of all the ages wouldn't fill it, and there

you'll be like a little bit of grit in the middle of the steppe.

Some critics have proposed that *Endgame* takes place in some postcatastrophic age and that these four figures, closed in a shelter, represent the only survivors. As Ruby Cohn notes, an early manuscript version of the work that slowly became *Fin de partie* and then *Endgame*, 'locates the shelter in Picardy, where destruction occurred "dans des circonstances mysterieuses" between 1914 and 1918'.[9] Beckett's specific reference indicates that he began to work on the play with a spatial vision that included an interior shelter within a ruined external landscape. However, in the processes of revision in which the play grew, the specificity of that relationship between interior and exterior disappeared. The sense of this enclosed space as a shelter exists only in the perception of Hamm and Clov; they use it as a shelter and envisage the external world as death.

Others have seen the interior space of the room that Beckett describes as the image of the interior of a skull with the two high windows as eyes looking out on the world. In that interpretation of the play Hamm and Clov function as aspects of a single psyche. Although in *Endgame* Beckett does focus more attention on Hamm than on Clov, the presence of Clov as a separate person is necessary. In this play Beckett reveals a character who goes through a series of exercises that enact his interpretations of the role or roles that constitute his being. In that sense, Hamm's behaviour is an existential performance. This performance, however, depends upon Clov's presence. Throughout the play the presence of Clov stimulates Hamm to imagine himself as the object of the servant's perception. While that perception confirms his sense of his own existence, it remains equivocal on at least two bases:

first of all, Clov is always an alien figure and, secondly, Clov perceives a performance rather than real behaviour. Hamm creates an image of himself for Clov – and thus for himself. Hamm's being is equivocal to the servant for whom he performs, to himself, and to the audience. The scene of *Endgame* cannot be the inside of Hamm's skull, the projection of his consciousness, because it must function as the neutral ground in which the protagonist plays himself and is perceived by the others for whom he performs.

Time

Even though the nature of the 'course' that is taking place in *Endgame* remains undefined, the play seems to imitate some inexorable movement from one point in time to another. Hamm's ambivalent attitude toward death – '. . . it's time it ended, . . . And yet I hesitate to . . . to end' – expresses a conflict between his desire to sustain speech with Clov and his desire to move towards the peaceful silence of death. Hamm's death may be immediately imminent as the play itself ends. If so, that termination of the action differs radically from the potential repetition of afternoons of waiting that seems to be the projected future of *Godot*.

The physical exercises that Beckett's characters perform and the words they speak represent behaviour fixed in habit. Each repetition plays within a range of variations but constitutes a unit within a sequence. Each event dramatised is unique only in that sense. Initially *Endgame* seems to differ from *Godot* as a representation of a single action within one segment of time. Each of the characters of *Endgame* suffers the consequences of age and the depletion of their world's resources. Hamm confronts those losses and attempts to accelerate his movement towards the death they signal. Whereas he experiences the absence, deterioration and consumption of certain physical objects on which he has depended for comfort, Hamm discards those that remain, and he seems to accommodate Clov's impending departure as he prepares himself for death. While Vladimir and Estragon perceive themselves trapped within the bounds of their relationship, they are not free to dissolve it. *Endgame*, however, offers the possibility that the relationship of Hamm and Clov is terminated.

I used the speculative phrase 'offers the possibility' because Beckett's plays do not produce meaning, but rather establish a series of indeterminacies which in turn play on the spectator's imagination and provoke a particular kind of speculation. Consequently, whereas I offer the proposition that *Endgame* may imitate the dissolution of the relationship of Hamm and Clov, I also identify the possibility that the play represents the imitation of an imitation: that Hamm and Clov are performing a 'set piece' in which Clov prepares for departure and Hamm prepares himself for death. If the latter interpretation is possible, *Endgame* exercises a notion of time similar to that in *Godot*; and the audience should consider the possibility that Hamm and Clov will, once again, resume their game.

Beckett establishes a critical indeterminacy in the early moments of the play at that point when Hamm assumes the *persona* of the actor and recites lines that assume the style of heroic drama:

HAMM: Me – (*he yawns*) – to play.

The lines which follow this opening statement consist of an

inflated theatrical speech. Hamm's personality here seems
to divide between the *persona* he imitates, the character
from the heroic drama, and his fundamental self who
comments upon the performance or, at least, the content
of the lines. For example:

> Can there be misery – (*he yawns*) – loftier than mine? No
> doubt.

As this passage continues, he continues to undercut his
own performance with ironic answers to his rhetorical
questions and, as well, with his yawning – a gesture that
suggests bored familiarity with the routine of this
performance. The section in which he speaks of ending
appears to be part of the theatrical recitation and should be
voiced within the elevated style of the performance,
punctuated by the yawning which manifests the attitude of
the basic *persona* of the character Hamm.

In the final section of *Endgame* Hamm calls for his
father and his son and he celebrates the fact that they do
not answer him, but Beckett frames this act by putting it
inside Hamm's recitation. This manipulation of the
character's voice suggests that Hamm's final renunciation
is not an experience unique to this moment but rather part
of a performance which he enacts periodically. The *project
of ending*, a performance of the movement towards death,
may be Hamm's fiction, an equivalent to the strategy of
waiting in *Godot*. Clov may well function as an accomplice
within the limits of that project although he maintains an
ironic perspective towards Hamm's role-playing. The
ultimate mystery of *Endgame* rests in the consciousness of
Clov. Is his pending departure the final movement of a
conventional game shared by the two, or is this day special,
the moment of his actual departure and Hamm's death?

Because the text itself provides no final clarification, the resolution of these questions can only occur in the imagination of the spectator. However, any fixed resolution violates the play. The characters that Beckett creates qualify each of their assertions with a statement or a gesture that directly or indirectly invalidates it. The pattern of proposition and denial, assertion and retraction, marks Beckett's writing at each stage of his work. As the protagonist of a Beckett work struggles with basic epistemological questions and attempts to confront the possibilities of his own knowledge, he recognises that for any proposition there is an equally valid denial. The omnipresent crisis in Beckett's fiction and drama derives from the character's realisation that he lives within the oscillation between that positive and that negative.

The tensions within the spectator's imagination that these contradictions set up reproduce, to some degree, the crisis experienced by the characters who live in Beckett's world. Wolfgang Iser's analysis of the nature of the spectator's response to *Endgame* describes this process well:

> . . . *Endgame* compels its spectator to reject the 'meanings' it stimulates, and in this way conveys something of the 'unendingness' of the end and the nature of the fictions which we are continually fabricating in order to finish off the end or to close the gaps in our own experiences. By compelling the spectator to reject the meaning he himself has suggested, *Endgame* offers a new experience, unique to the world of literature, in which one is enabled to penetrate below the surface of one's own meaning projections and to gain insight into those factors that guide the individual in his personal mode of interpretation.[10]

'Endgame'

Beckett's unequivocal refusal to discuss his plays, clarify intentions or comment upon the meaning of his work must derive from his own awareness that the significance of his dramas depends upon their exercise of indeterminacies, not from their representation of experience that can be translated into interpretations of human behaviour. The radical simplicity of the environments he creates and the ambiguous nature of the time he imitates force his spectators to confront the very uncertainties that plague the minds of his characters.

Samuel Beckett's theatre builds images of character, space and time that embody antitheses. *Endgame*, as the dramas that follow it, imitates the process of dying; but it *performs* a gesture of ending, it does not necessarily enact one. My argument suggests a circular structure in which the ending of the play implies the possibility of another beginning. Shortly after *Endgame* begins Clov uncovers Hamm who immediately initiates a bored performance of a play-within-a-play, and *Endgame* ends within the same mode of an internal performance.

The principal figures of *Molloy* and *Malone Dies* are writers. Each of these characters, with Mahood in *The Unnamable*, approach the act of writing or spinning fictions with a keen self-consciousness. As they recognise, the products they create have authenticity only as writing. That is, their stories do not document a reality apart from the process of writing itself. By establishing the fact that his protagonists are writers, Beckett creates a world in the novels that is wholly self-contained. The only reality to which these writers refer is the text of their writing. The novels do not imitate reality; they imitate writing.

Like Vladimir and Estragon in *Godot*, Hamm and Clov are aware of their status as actors in a theatre. When he turns his telescope towards the audience, Clov acknowledges the nature of the spectators who watch *Endgame*:

> I see . . . a multitude . . . in transports . . . of joy.
> (*Pause*) That's what I call a magnifier.

Clov's comic inflation of both the size and the mood of the audience confirms his own function as a performer. His awareness of his presence in the theatre as an actor encompasses a realisation that this performance is only one unit in a series of performances – that the existence of *Endgame* as an aesthetic event is subject to an innumerable series of repetitions. Even if the audience assumes that the death of Hamm is going to take place immediately following the performance and imagines that Clov's departure is authentic, these same spectators know that Clov will uncover Hamm at the beginning of the next performance and continue to do so during *Endgame's* life as a play.

4
'All that Fall'

In 1956 the BBC commissioned Samuel Beckett to write a script suitable for radio production, and the playwright set to work on the text that became *All that Fall*.[1] The play, which was initially broadcast on the Third Programme in January 1957, marks Beckett's return to English; and here he uses specifically Irish characters moving through a familiar Irish landscape.

The play concerns an old couple, Maddy and Dan Rooney, the woman ill, obese and garrulous, the old man blind, ill and taciturn. Beckett uses a simple organisational scheme to structure the drama: Maddy Rooney journeys on foot to meet her husband, Dan, who arrives on the up-mail, a train from town, and leads the blind man home. The play divides into three principal sections: the journey to the depot, the wait for the train that arrives after an unexpected delay, and the return. The first two sections concentrate upon the character of Maddy, and the third balances the characters of the failing old couple as they struggle labouriously on the road towards home. As in

Waiting for Godot and *Endgame*, Beckett builds his drama on the base of a relationship between two old people, but here – in the division of focus among the sections – it is possible to see the exploration of a single character in space which marks the plays that succeed *All that Fall*.

Maddy, 'a lady in her seventies', is an obese creature weighing 'two hundred pounds of unhealthy fat', if we can believe her blind husband. Her flesh constitutes a physical burden which almost immobilises her, and that burden is balanced with the emotional weight of the memory of her daughter's death, some forty or fifty years in the past. Her hysterical response to that memory periodically halts her in the roadway, bowing her over mentally and physically:

> How can I go on, I cannot. Oh let me just flop down flat on the road like a big fat jelly out of a bowl and never move again! A great big slop thick with grit and dust and flies, they would have to scoop me up with a shovel.

She sees herself imprisoned in her flesh, and in this state of consciousness she longs for freedom from her body. The event of Minnie's death forms the principal image of Maddy Dunne Rooney's consciousness, and in the forty to fifty years that have passed since then, she has neither accommodated nor resolved that experience.

Ironically, in *All that Fall*, a drama that exists only as language and sound, Beckett uses language to hide the presence of a memory that cannot be spoken but remains in consciousness. Maddy's periodic references to Minnie signal the presence of that memory but do not explicate it. She sees herself, however, held captive in both her flesh and her memories. She speaks of a fantasy of illness which reveals that perception:

. . . just wasting slowly painlessly away, keeping up my strength with arrowroot and calves-foot jelly, till in the end you wouldn't see me under the blankets any more than a board. . . . just drifting gently down into the higher life, and remembering, remembering, . . . (*the voice breaks*) . . . all the silly unhappiness . . . as though . . . it had never happened . . . .

While this statement demonstrates her desire to dissolve both mind and body, she persists in holding onto life, using this day as a specific event. Despite her illness and obesity, the anniversary of her husband's birth motivates her to meet him at Bogshill herself rather than use the services of young Jerry who regularly leads him home. She longs for the presence and the affection of her husband, and the relationship to him provides the thin thread of her connection to this world: 'Love, that is all I asked . . . .'

Maddy is surrounded, on the road and at the station, by a variety of village types – Christy, a carter; Mr Tyler, a retired bill-broker, who is hurrying to the races; Mr Slocum, Clerk of the Racecourse; Tommy, a porter; the irritable Mr Barrell, station-master; the devout spinster, Miss Fitt; and an unidentified woman and small girl. Beckett's brief and pointed characterisations of these people are satiric but not bitter. Their function is more scenic than personal, in a sense, since their repeated welcome and then alienation from Maddy form a pattern. As Maddy says,

I estrange them all. They come towards me, uninvited, bygones bygones, full of kindness, anxious to help . . . (*the voice breaks*) . . . genuinely pleased . . . to see me again . . . looking so well . . . . (*Handkerchief*) A few simple words . . . from my heart . . . and I am all alone

. . . once more . . . . (*Handkerchief. Vehemently*) I should not be out at all! I should never leave the grounds!

Maddy's language, her excessive, strange and hyperbolic speech in combination with her aggressive demands for help seem to distance them. She sees herself separated from her language. In this way she faces the basic epistemological problem indirectly. The language she uses appears to her to be archaic, disconnected from the events, objects and people of the world she knows. She questions Christy, her first companion on the road to Bogshill Station:

Do you find anything . . . bizarre about my way of speaking? (*Pause*) I do not mean the voice. (*Pause*) No, I mean the words. (*Pause. More to herself*) I use none but the simplest words, I hope, and yet I sometimes find my way of speaking very . . . bizarre.

As they trudge home, Dan questions her phrase, 'safe to haven', and comments that she appears to be 'struggling with a dead language'. She agrees, and he confesses that he feels the same way about his own speech on those occasions when he overhears it.

Dan Rooney, blind and infirm, seems older than Maddy. He forgets that this day is his birthday, despite her morning greeting and gift. He asks if he is a hundred. Maddy doesn't know and announces there is no one to ask. When she asks him if he is well, he responds in a lengthy and comic chronicle of his infirmities, ending with the ironic comment:

No, I cannot be said to be well. But I am no worse. The

loss of my sight was a great fillip. If I could go deaf and blind I think I might pant on to be a hundred. Or have I done so?

Rooney's fantasy of deafness and muteness balances Maddy's description of a dissolution out of flesh. Both picture a solipsistic silence, and yet they cling to each other on their journey towards home, 'safe to haven'.

Beckett's characterisation of Rooney is problematic. At the end of the play the listening audience learns that the incident on the train that caused its late arrival was an accident in which a young child was killed by falling under the wheels. Earlier in the play Rooney confesses to a desire to kill a child. He asks Maddy: 'Did you ever wish to kill a child? (*Pause*) Nip some young doom in the bud.' In a manuscript version of the play, the line is more specifically pointed; he says: 'I should like to kill a child before I die. A little girl.'[2] When, at the end of the play we learn that a child has been killed on the train, it is necessary to rethink the whole course of Rooney's dialogue with his wife – speech which has aimed to hide the very incident that dominates his consciousness.

Scene

Beckett visualises his dramatic characters in some form of spatial confinement. Vladimir and Estragon seem compelled to station themselves near the single tree that distinguishes the particular section of the barren plain of the Cackon country that the audience sees. Hamm and Clov are bound to their shelter, and if Clov leaves it may well be to his death. Beckett may not identify these restrictive environments geographically or historically, but he clarifies their boundaries and suggests that his protagonists could not exist apart from the places they inhabit.

In her discussion of Beckett's work as a director, Ruby Cohn quotes a statement made by the playwright and included in Michael Haerdter's *Materialien zu Becketts Endspiel*:

> For me theatre is first of all a relaxation from work on fiction. We are dealing with a definite space and people in this space. That's relaxing.[3]

This statement relates to Beckett's claim, cited earlier, that he began writing plays as a diversion from his problems with prose. In fiction the words alone establish the sense of place. In the theatre the playwright begins with an image of space created by the physical reality of the stage itself. A dramatist can, of course, define or restrict that space at will; and, in the course of performance, reveal both the quality of the site and the character's perception of it. The theatre offers the writer what the novel cannot: the simultaneous presence of the image of place and the character's perception of it. The scenographic image – the barren stretch of ground in *Godot*, the sheltering walls of *Endgame* – provides a clear visual field in which the spectator sees the character throughout the performance. As the character struggles with the difficulties of perceiving himself in that field, attempting to gain a clear relationship to that place, the psychological distance between the character and the space he inhabits grows into a dominant image. As the character uses the space, imposing his habits upon it, the site becomes familiar to him. The scenic image of *Godot*, the barren field with its single tree, transforms a bare stage into the image of equivocal space that Beckett creates. Vladimir and

Estragon move into that place and re-form it into an improvised stage for their routines. Yet, because these activities are imposed upon the site, it always remains an alien ground for them.

The fixed sites in which Beckett situates the characters of each dramatic work discipline the texts and the performance of them. The character's use of memory or invention begins with an awareness of the place he presently inhabits, accepting its unfamiliarity and hostility. As the character proceeds to impose another reality upon it – the tramps' routines and verbal games, Hamm's performance – the spectator perceives the difference between the mental images that direct their behaviour and the physical presence of the site itself. The characters' memories or inventions, juxtaposed to the authentic image of the place that holds them, become ephemeral, even archaic, as they refer to an earlier world or objects and places more complex and detailed than the world formed by the present scene.

While Beckett endows the site of the drama with an authenticity that derives from its actual presence, he undermines that authenticity by his refusal to locate that space in any context other than its immediate presence. Part of Beckett's process of revision includes the gradual elimination of details that would situate the action of the plays in a specific context – geographical and historical.[4] Because the specific identity of the place remains indeterminate, the basic epistemological question suffered by the character has no solution – either for him or for the spectator. To perceive the actuality of the site would be an affirmation of the possibility of knowledge. The plays project the increasing separation of character and scene; the scenic space may be the place that confines him and provides the field in which we see the character, but his

81

image of that place or of himself within it has no more verifiable authenticity than his images of the past because neither can be tested. In that sense, the image of place in Beckett's plays maintains both presence and indeterminacy.

In radio drama, of course, the playwright does not have the physical resources of actual space. Words and sounds must create a sense of location. Beckett's stage plays depend upon the presence of the physical site in his representation of the irredeemable psychological distance between character and scene. In this first radio drama Beckett presents an analogous division in the process of differentiating the scenic sounds and the character's perception and response. For example, Beckett introduces the listener to the rural scene of *All that Fall* with a series of sounds – sheep, bird, cow, cock, heard individually and then in chorus – but Maddy perceives her journey through that pastoral landscape as a painful pilgrimage through some hostile territory. For both the Rooneys, the landscape is strewn with signs of death. Using biblical references which are typical of her, Maddy sees herself within the dust of mortality:

> Let us halt a moment and this vile dust fall back upon the viler worms. . . . I am not half alive nor anything approaching it. (*Pause*) What are we standing here for? This dust will not settle in our time.

Rooney identifies them with Dante's damned couple, suggesting that they proceed on their journey '. . . you forwards and I backwards. The perfect pair. Like Dante's damned with their faces arsy-versy. Our tears will water our bottoms.'

While he organises the drama in the form of a journey,

allowing for a progression of scenic images rather than a single site, Beckett builds the spatial image of a circular course: the roadway past the house in which the record of 'Death and the Maiden' plays continually, past the laburnum bushes, to the station with its 'Matterhorn' of steps, from the station, down the steps, past the laburnum to the old house, past the house to the site, apparently, at which the play began. The spatial images external to the course – the town from which the up-mail travels, even the home towards which they travel – become vague locations, remaining just outside the sharp focus in which that course is perceived. While the image of the road is linear, the movement within the extended site Beckett creates is circular. Within that circularity, however, Beckett's characters move into an increasingly hostile world. The 'lovely day for the races' transforms itself into a stormy afternoon with rain and biting winds: 'I feel very cold and faint. The wind – *whistling wind* – is whistling through my summer frock as if I had nothing on over my bloomers.' When Rooney stops and Maddy tells him where he is, 'bowed down over the ditch', Rooney tells her there is a dead dog in the vicinity. Maddy, for him and for the listeners, tells him that it is the smell of rotting leaves. When Rooney protests, 'In June? Rotting leaves in June?' she replies: 'Yes dear, from last year, and from the year before last, and from the year before that again.' Rather than identifying the cycles of nature in patterns of regeneration, Maddy sees the evidence of nature as the accumulation of dead things.

Maddy and Dan Rooney not only move into a steadily increasing storm as they progress on their laborious passage homeward, they also move into an isolated world. After the departure of the Lynch twins and before the wind begins, Maddy observes: 'All is still. No living soul in sight.' Their journey home contrasts dynamically with her walk to Bogshill when the road was well-travelled by others. Beckett isolates them on a wind- and rain-swept road.

Time

As he develops the spatial image that encloses the action of *All that Fall*, Beckett establishes its literal temporal structure clearly: the performance encompasses Maddy Rooney's journey from some undetermined point on the road between her home and the Bogshill depot to meet her blind husband when he disembarks from the late train, and extends to the point at which they arrive at the place on the road at which the play began. The train, the up-mail, is due from town at 12:30, and shortly after she arrives at Bogshill, Maddy notes that it is 12:36. The train finally arrives, fifteen minutes late on a thirty-minute course. Dan Rooney's comments establish that the day is Saturday, 'the intermission' from work when he, apparently, leaves his office at noon rather than five. Early in the performance the listeners learn that it is a day of the races, Mr Slocum, Clerk of the Racecourse, hoists the heavy Maddy into his car when he finds her on the road. This particular day is also special because it is Dan Rooney's birthday.

The playwright marks the sequence of Maddy's journey with a series of *stations*, identifying landmarks of a sort that, when they make their return journey, will show their movement through space and time: first of all, Maddy's dragging feet stop at the sound of Schubert's 'Death and the Maiden', which, she points out, comes from 'a ruinous old house' inhabited solely by an old woman; she also, further along the road, notes the smell of the poisonous shrub laburnum; she experiences a period of immobility;

and, after her lift in Mr Slocum's automobile, she painfully ascends the steps leading from the public road to the platform. After the time spent waiting for the train and Dan's arrival, the pair undertake the difficult journey back toward their home: the laborious descent of the steps, a period of immobility, the smell of laburnum and the sound of Schubert's music, this time specifically identified by Dan as 'Death and the Maiden'. The play ends, as it began, with the shuffling of feet coming to a halt – with the addition here of the sound of the wind and the rain.

The journey, meeting and return journey in *All that Fall* constitute the plot, whereas the embedded narrative projects an image of extended suffering, marked at the beginning and end by the death of a child. Beckett's narrative, radically reduced in detail, reveals no sequential history, but focuses on these two events: one that possesses the consciousness of Maddy Rooney and the other that dominates the consciousness of Dan Rooney even though its nature remains hidden until the final moment of the play. Neither Maddy nor Dan describe these deaths nor put them into a context; Beckett's exposition of these events remains indirect; he dramatises the suffering that is the manifestation of the event. Maddy's consciousness returns again and again to the image of her dead child.

(*Sobbing*) Minnie! Little Minnie! . . . (*Brokenly*) In her forties now she'd be, I don't know, fifty, girding up her lovely little loins, getting ready for the change . . . .

Beckett establishes the general time-frame for Minnie's death and, with bitter irony, compounds that image of death with Maddy's recognition that if her daughter had lived, she would be at the point of menopause.

The second death remains undisclosed until the final

moment of the play. As the collection of villagers wait for the late up-mail, the reason for its delay remains a mystery. Dan refuses to discuss the fifteen-minute stop *en route*, claiming that he has no idea why the train stopped. After they have passed the house with the continual playing of 'Death and the Maiden', Jerry – the young boy who usually leads the blind Rooney home – catches up with the couple in order to give the old man an object, a ball-like round thing which he dropped. Against the man's objections, the boy tells Mrs Rooney what delayed the train:

JERRY: It was a little child, Ma'am. (*Mr Rooney groans*)
MRS ROONEY: What do you mean, it was a little child?
JERRY: It was a little child fell out of the carriage, onto the line, Ma'am. (*Pause*) Under the wheels, Ma'am.

The audience hears the sound of Jerry's departure, the wind and the rain, its abating, the dragging steps of the silent old couple as they continue on their course, their halting, the resumption of the wind and the rain; and the drama is closed.

Beckett builds the sense of an implied narrative through a series of subtly worked connections among units of the text. For example, the early presence of Schubert's music provides a suggestive image to those who recognise the composition as 'Death and the Maiden'. Maddy's reference to the woman – 'All alone in that ruinous old house' – points toward an image of a woman grieving over the death of a daughter. When Maddy makes reference to the death of her own daughter, the listener's imagination returns to the musical image, reforming that moment in which Maddy comments upon the loneliness of the old woman. Now the listener can perceive Maddy's sympathetic statement as her identification with the situation of the sorrowing mother who manifests her grief by listening to music that represents it. In turn, Mr Tyler's reference to his daughter's hysterectomy, leaving him 'grandchildless', can be seen, in retrospect as a particularly painful item of news to Maddy when, shortly afterwards, she mourns her own childlessness. Even the interspersed voice of the woman as the train arrives, outlining a potential accident, contributes to the building of a compound image of the death of daughters, childlessness and sterility:

Come, Dolly darling, let us take up our stand before the first-class smokers. Give me your hand, one can be sucked under.

When the woman speaks this line, it seems to be a contribution to the generalised metaphoric model of dead children. At the final moment of *All that Fall*, however, that line may be remembered as a careful preparation for the accident that, in a reconstructed narrative, has happened prior to the train's arrival and her statement.

Beckett postpones the explanation of the train's delay until the final moment of the play. Rooney refuses to discuss it despite the persistence and emotionality of Maddy's questioning. Immediately after her final request, they encounter the jeers of the Lynch twins. The hostility of these children, who earlier pelted them with mud, reinforces the basic image of childnessness both in its presentation of children as alien to the Rooneys and in the way it provokes the following exchange:

MRS ROONEY: Let us turn and face them. (*Cries. They turn*)

MR ROONEY: Did you ever wish to kill a child? (*Pause*)

Nip some young doom in the bud. (*Pause*) Many a time at night, in winter, on the black road home, I nearly attacked the boy! (*Pause*) Poor Jerry!

Perhaps consideration of himself as a possible child-murderer stimulates his proposal that they proceed in the position of Dante's dead couple; or perhaps, as the listener may speculate later, he imagines himself in the inferno because of his responsibility for the child's death on the train.

In a few moments he begins to tell Maddy of the journey, explaining that he used the time of the trip from town to Bogshill to consider the possibility of retirement. When he spoke of his periodic desire to kill Jerry, he asked himself: 'What restrained me then? (*Pause*) Not fear of man.' As he describes his behaviour on the train, he states: 'I had the compartment to myself, as usual. At least I hope so, for I made no attempt to restrain myself.' Beckett builds a narrative structure based on indeterminancy, provoking several questions: (1) Is the recitation about retirement a strategy to deflect Maddy from her insistence upon learning the truth of the delay? (2) Is it a relatively authentic account of Rooney's thought processes? (3) Is it a rationalisation for his decision not to return to town because of the trauma he experienced in being a hearing witness to the child's death or a participant in that event? Is his lack of restraint during this journey an indication that he is the cause of that death?

When he gives his possibly fictitious account of the journey from town to Bogshill, Maddy has no reply. She will not assert that she believes him. At this point, however, she herself begins to tell a story, the report of the lecture by the 'new mind doctor' who speaks about 'a little girl, very strange and unhappy in her ways, and how he treated her unsuccessfully over a period of years and was finally obliged to give up the case'. Deirdre Bair reports that in the autumn of 1935 Carl Jung delivered a series of five lectures at the Tavistock Clinic and that Samuel Beckett attended the third. These lectures, published under the title *Analytic Psychology, Its Theory and Practice*, provided the anecdote about the little girl which obsesses Maddy. She cites 'the mind doctor', isolating the comment that causes her to spend sleepless nights brooding 'On it and other wretchedness':

> . . . he suddenly raised his head and exclaimed, as if he had had a revelation, The trouble with her was she had never been really born!

Jung's words are close: 'She had never been born entirely.'[5]

In this sequence Rooney's recitation of his passage on the train, which omits the central incident, is answered by another recitation which reports the strange death of a young girl. In a few moments Jerry catches up with them and corrects Dan Rooney's account of the sequence of events on the train. This revised version of the delay causes the listener to rework the previous behaviour of Dan Rooney in the imagination. This incident, a fresh and recent death, is the climax to the series of images of the death of children, childlessness and sterility which have accumulated.

It is possible to perceive *All that Fall* outside narrative terms, seeing the work as a sequence of images, subtly interwoven and held together within a minimal plot. However, the embedded or implicit narrative of *All that Fall*, despite its critical indeterminacies, does constitute a principal communicative function in the work. Northrop

Frye uses the Greek term, *anagnorisis*, which Aristotle employs to identify the moment of the hero's recognition of some specific fact, to define an experience in the spectator's imagination. The moment of *anagnorisis*, in Frye's sense, is that point in the literary work at which the reader (or spectator) understands the general shape of the narrative and can predict its disposition.[6] Beckett confounds that experience, delaying that moment until the end of the performance of *All that Fall.* The play closes with the sounds of dragging feet progressing then halting as the sound of the storm increases in volume. The listener's recognition, which must come as a surprise, jeopardises his previous 'interpretation' of the action and one of its two principal characters. In this final moment, the listener revises his sense of the preceding action and formulates an image of a narrative that extends from the death of Minnie Rooney to the death of the young child, perhaps another young girl, on the train. As well, perhaps, the alert listener recognises that the second critical event, the train accident, probably occurred during the time of performance as Maddy Rooney trudges towards Bogshill Station.

The repetitious variants of the image of the dead child are not merely part of a poetic or static organisation. While they do build that kind of a structure, these images also provide the equivalent of the text that haunts the consciousness of Beckett's other heroes. Maddy cannot free herself from the memory of Minnie's death, and its presence within her consciousness forces her to see her present in terms of that critical fact of her past. Dan Rooney's consciousness, also haunted by the image of a child's death, focuses on displaced images of that incident, avoiding speaking about it directly – for reasons that Beckett elects not to disclose.

'All that Fall'

Critics frequently note the absence of narrative in Beckett's plays, describing them as expanded moments or dramatisations of a single image. Obviously, Beckett presents characters outside the context of a psychological history, but each of his characters responds to an image of the past and, obliquely and indirectly, Beckett reveals fragments of that past. That past, as any other data with which the character works, is equivocal, enigmatic and unverifiable. However, these fragments, forming an implicit narrative that is dim in outline and, ultimately, inpenetrable, constitute a theatrical presence that, in juxtaposition to the physical presence of the site, determines the situation of the character.

5
'Krapp's Last Tape'

Samuel Beckett was intrigued with the sound of Patrick Magee's voice when he met the actor who played Mr Slocum in the BBC production of *All that Fall*. Deirdre Bair reports that Beckett told Magee that his voice was the one he heard as he wrote. Beckett decided to write a play for the Irish actor; the original notebook manuscript of *Krapp's Last Tape* is titled 'Magee Monologue'. Following his usual routine, the playwright then produced a series of typescripts working toward the final text of the play as published.[1] This new work opened the bill in the production of *Endgame* at the Royal Court in October 1958, with Magee playing the role written for him.

Krapp's Last Tape develops Beckett's notion of the relationship between the present and the images of the past that inhabit consciousness. Beckett's work invariably includes stories that evoke a sense of the past and employs physical objects that function as relics of a previous time. Malone, for example, recounts his tales and inventories his possessions as a method of dealing with the experience of dying. The process of making an inventory offers Beckett's characters the satisfaction of being able to verify some aspect of their reality, but the authenticity of these things is subject to the same kind of epistemological questioning that everything in Beckett's world undergoes. The act of inventorying an object and describing its presence gives his characters the opportunity to establish a model of subject and object in their imagination. Speaking of the self in relationship to an object sustains an image of the self both as the perceiving subject and as the speaker. Speech provides Beckett's heroes with the means to maintain their self-consciousness, and the presence of objects to discuss assists that project. The final inventory aims to renounce the object and move into silence, the silence that seems to loom just beyond the moment when the text ends or the performance closes. In *Endgame*, for example, each of the objects for which Hamm calls is significant to him as a stimulus to speech. He discards these things as he renounces language.

When Beckett's creatures tell their stories and discuss the objects in their possession, they act as both speaker and principal listener. The novel offered Beckett the convention of the first-person narrative in which the protagonist himself writes the text that constitutes the book, making the presence of another character, as listener, unnecessary. In his first group of plays he needs to include other characters to provide the protagonist with the occasion for speech. The physical device of the tape-recorder allows Beckett to return to the image of the solitary figure. The separate voice of the younger Krapp combined with the presence of the older figure who listens completes the paradigm. The text spoken by the recorded voice also becomes the principal physical object the hero possesses, the tangible relic of the past as part of the collection of tapes. The tapes are both text and object. They have an immediacy and authenticity that Beckett's other relics of the past do not have, but their physical separation from Krapp and his enigmatic response to them demonstrates the gap between past and present. The gap is both spatial and psychological. In *Krapp's Last Tape* Beckett uses images of space and character to examine problems in the perception of time.

Time

Beckett's dramatic economy reduces the literal time of his plays to a brief segment of his protagonist's experience. He contrives, however, to represent a single moment and, simultaneously, to create a sense of extended time. In this play Beckett establishes the time as a precise moment: the hero's sixty-ninth birthday. He develops an image of an extensive past in the form of the boxes of recording tape that ostensibly house years of memories. His ledger suggests a compulsive record-keeping and functions as an image of collected moments in time. Krapp reads entries from this ledger which, as we recognise later, form quotations from the tape he has chosen to play.

As Krapp plays the tape we recognise that the antithesis of light and dark informs each of the three segments. In the scene that marks the death of his mother the voice of the younger Krapp notes the black and white costume of the nursemaid in the park, her dark beauty and the funereal 'black hooded perambulator'. The critical image of seeing the lowered blind in the window of his mother's room, signifying her death, also suggests a tension between light and darkness. 'Memorable . . . Equinox' refers to the moment in March when he stands at the end of the jetty confronting the storm. At the point of the Equinox the day and the night are of equal length, darkness and light in perfect balance. The taped voice speaks of a moment of clear recognition:

> What I suddenly saw then was this, that the belief I had been going on all my life, namely – (*Krapp switches off impatiently, winds tape forward, switches on again*) – great granite rocks the foam flying up in the light of the lighthouse and the wind-gauge spinning like a propeller, clear to me at last that the dark I have always struggled to keep under is in reality my most – (*Krapp curses, switches off, . . .*).

In the storm he confronts the presence of darkness within his own being that he had 'struggled to keep under'.

In Beckett, lighted space, marking off the surrounding darkness, always suggests self-awareness. The light illuminates the self as an imagined object within its own perception. In the performance of the play, Krapp balances his time between the illuminated circle in which his table sits and the darkness into which he periodically disappears. He forces himself back into the light in order to confront the memories and images of himself. The light illuminates the self as an object within its own perception. During the course of the performance, Krapp retreats into the darkness, forcing himself to move back into the light to confront the memories and the images of the self that are contained in the tapes.

In the third principal memory – the scene in the boat – Krapp also focuses on the tension between the light and the dark. Here the scene is filled with brilliant sunlight. He describes the woman in the punt:

> She lay stretched out on the floorboards with her hands

under her head and her eyes closed. Sun blazing down, bit of a breeze, water nice and lively. . . . I asked her to look at me and after a few moments – (*pause*) – after a few moments – (*pause*) – after a few moments she did, but the eyes just slits, because of the glare. I bent over her to get them in the shadow and they opened. (*Pause. Low*) Let me in.

Krapp's reference is, surely, sexual. However, the plea to let him in seems to refer, as well, to her perception of him. Shielded from the sun, she can open her eyes to encompass his image and, in that sense, acknowledge his being and his presence. Seeing himself reflected in her eyes confirms his identity. Although this memory recounts the dissolution of their relationship, his desire to be seen by her demonstrates his ambivalence.

Whereas Beckett invests the three incidents that the recording discusses with a detail which is rare for this playwright, he fragments the ostensibly complete tape, omitting portions of the message and presenting the recollection of the year's experience without continuity or context. Consequently, what remains constitutes a series of graphic details that do not form a conventional narrative because the relationship among the events remains unclarified. For example: did Krapp's reaction to his mother's death in the autumn lead him to an analysis of his own life that, in turn, produced the vision he experienced on the jetty during the storm in the following spring? Did that self-knowledge, then, motivate him to dissolve his relationship to the woman in the boat sometime in the summer? These questions which the play may provoke in the spectator's imagination would be external to Beckett's play except that the absence of their answers forms gaps in the image of Krapp's consciousness. Krapp himself revolves these specific segments of the year in his mind without assimilating them or synthesising them into a coherent narrative.

Beckett's plays never enact a story. They present a character repeating the text of a story, usually partial and disjunctively organised, perhaps for the last time. Beckett's particular use of the image of the past as the material with which a character struggles in the present is not an idiosyncratic method of organising a dramatic action. Sophocles' *Oedipus Tyrannus* presents the image of the king responding to the oblique form of Creon's report from the Apollonian oracle in Delphi and reveals the hero gradually revising his understanding of the words of the oracle he received as a youth in Corinth. *Hamlet* dramatises the prince's efforts to accommodate the story he hears from the figure of his father's ghost. Macbeth rebuilds his life to match the telegraphed description of its course that he hears from the witches. In these tragedies, of course, the text that the hero plays in his mind and attempts to resolve is revealed to him within a clear historical context. Beckett, on the other hand, reduces the action of his dramas to the recitation of that text in the hero's mind. As the hero responds to the information the text provides, he recognises that nothing can be verified other than the presence of the text in his consciousness. The words, however, are familiar to him, suggesting that the text has inhabited his mind for an extended period of time.

Beckett's plays suggest that the specific repetition dramatised in the play is only one in a series. In the eighth of *Texts for Nothing* a voice says: '. . . it's for ever the same murmur, flowing and unbroken, like a single endless word and therefore meaningless, for it's the end gives meaning to words.'[2] This concept suggests that the final repetition of the text in the character's consciousness will bring, at last, a sense of its significance. It may be tempting to think that Beckett's practice of representing situations in which a character, apparently near the end of his life, engages in some retrospective inventory of objects and memories, represents a search for the kind of meaning possible at the end. Krapp, however, cannot organise his sense of experience in a kind of comprehensive vision. As he records his 'last' tape, we recognise that his ability to frame his experience in words at sixty-nine is radically inferior to his skill at thirty-nine. His present recording suggests both the limitations of his present experience and the limitations of his ability to speak about it. He abandons the project and returns again to the earlier recording, playing the incident with the woman in the boat for the third time and the *ending* of that tape:

> *Pause. Krapp's lips move. No sound.* Past midnight. Never knew such silence. The earth might be uninhabited. *Pause.* Here I end this reel. Box – (*pause*) – three, spool – (*pause*) – five. (*Pause*) Perhaps my best years are gone. When there was a chance of happiness. But I wouldn't want them back. Not with the fire in me now. No, I wouldn't want them back. *Krapp motionless staring before him. The tape runs on in silence.*

With the stage direction *'Krapp's lips move'*, Beckett suggests that the old man's familiarity with the words of this tape allows him to accompany it with subvocalised speech so that he speaks as well as hears the tape – the words of the past providing the substance of his present consciousness. The close of the early tape becomes the ending of the play itself, the voice of the thirty-nine-year-old Krapp speaking the words appropriate for the sixty-nine-year-old who, in turn, speaks them to himself. This statement of renunciation serves as well for this ending as it did for the earlier. At the final moment, therefore, the spectators perceive the image of the earlier Krapp experiencing the earlier ending, once again, as the ending to the present moment. The collection of tapes themselves provide a compound image of endings since these anniversary messages take the form of retrospective summaries that look back to the preceding year rather than ahead to the new year. *Krapp's Last Tape* projects a sense of time as a series of endings. The tapes themselves are endings, and the three sections of the tape Krapp plays enact endings.

The notion of life as a pattern of recurrent endings informs a short prose piece that Beckett wrote in the sixties but did not publish until 1976. 'For To End Yet Again' tells a cryptic story of two white figures who carry an almost lifeless body on a litter across a dusty plain. Despite the fact this character's death seems imminent, the text appears to rehearse the impossibility of ending, clarifying both the potential of a series of endings and the narrator's acute desire for an *absolute* end: 'Through it who knows yet another end beneath a cloudless sky same dark it earth and sky of a last end if ever there had to be another absolutely had to be.'[3] Beckett consistently avoids resolving his works with an absolute close; but here the voice who speaks asserts a keen desire for a 'last end', a desire that remains unrealised. His writing, including *Endgame* and *Krapp's Last Tape*, consistently plays with the notion of ending, not with the act of ending.

The language of 'For To End Yet Again' presents the possibility of an endless progression of deaths. Beckett avoids the representation of a clean termination that would be a release from the pain of the experience his creatures suffer or an eschatological destruction that would suggest the possibility of a new beginning. 'For To End Yet Again' is not to begin again but to experience yet again the process of ending. We do not know how many endings are ahead for Krapp.

Scene

The scenic image Beckett describes in *Krapp's Last Tape* appears to be simple: a table with two drawers, on its surface a tape-recorder, boxes holding reels of magnetic tape, and a microphone. While this interior space matches the bareness of the room described in *Endgame*, no walls are visible in *Krapp's Last Tape*. The even grey light that exposes the dimensions of the room in which Clov serves Hamm is replaced here with a 'strong white light' that illuminates only the area of the table and the space immediately adjacent. In *Endgame* Beckett establishes a keen difference between the room, as refuge, and the world external to that space. Even though the nature of the exterior landscape is equivocal in *Endgame*, the well-defined walls separate the room from some kind of hostile world. The specific nature of its presence remains unknowable, but the threat of the world on the other side of the walls of the 'shelter' is omnipresent. At this moment in their history the relationship of Hamm and Clov is bound to this room, and they perceive that in 'the . . . other hell' 'Outside of here it's death.' Hamm and Clov use the physical dimensions of the room, defined by the walls, with precision and clarity, and they frequently draw attention to the world without, especially at those moments when Clov climbs the ladder and looks out with his telescope. By contrast, the interior dimensions of the room that Krapp inhabits are indistinct. Here Beckett establishes a special tension, not between interior and exterior, but between light and darkness.

Beckett schedules Krapp's movement in and out of the darkness purposely. In the darkness he drinks; in the light he confronts the presence of an earlier Krapp as the tape has recorded him. Using this circle of light he also attempts to complete this year's 'retrospective'. Both anniversary messages note his movement between this private world and a public world external to this space, and he clearly sees his den as a refuge. Krapp's excursions into the public world, however, also mark his isolation. The three incidents on the earlier tape deal either with the termination of relationships or with moments of solitude. Even the references to the Winehouse and the park include the notation: 'Not a soul'. Rather than the opposition of public and private, interior and exterior, Beckett establishes a conflict between antithetical desires: to lose the self in darkness and to confront the self in the light.

The schematic opposition of light and darkness provides the dominant scenic element of this play, signalling the principal antithesis operating in Krapp's consciousness: the desire to continue his relentless examination and notation of his self and his desire to be free of the burden of these collected records; the desire to continue living within the sound of these recorded tapes or to be able to move into peaceful silence, completing the 'last' tape. The voice of the younger Krapp remarks on the installation of the light thirty years earlier:

Good to be back in my den, in my old rags. . . . The new light above my table is a great improvement. With all this darkness round me I feel less alone. (*Pause*) In a way. (*Pause*) I love to get up and move about in it, then back here to . . . (*hesitates*) . . . me. (*Pause*) Krapp.

As always in Beckett, the lighted space is not only a physical location but also an area in which the character can imagine himself or herself being seen. The darkness offers the character the opportunity to move away from this self-image and lose self-consciousness. Ultimately death promises darkness and the loss of the self. In the production of *Krapp's Last Tape* that Beckett directed at the Akademie der Kunste in Berlin he expanded two specific moments, adding what he called the Hain-play, a sequence of movements in which Krapp senses the presence of a benevolent death behind him in the darkness.[4] Immediately after he reads the ledger and just before the final playing of the passage about the woman in the boat, Krapp responds to this presence and then turns his attention to the light and the words on the tape. Here Beckett provides a clear indication of Krapp's antithetical desires: his longing for death, darkness and silence in tension with his need to sustain his consciousness of himself as the subject of the text he plays.

From the base provided by the division between light and darkness, the tape ranges into other imaginative locations with detailed graphic description that is more like the novels than the earlier plays. The memories that Vladimir and Estragon recount and the details of the past to which Hamm and Clov allude are expressed in phrases that sound removed from the events they recall, phrases that have been repeated so frequently and for such an extended period of time that detail has eroded. In *Krapp's Last Tape* we confront the undiminished, unattenuated original text. These memories are fresh, grounded in specific physical detail: the dark-eyed nurse in the park watching him as he stares at the window of the room in which his mother is dying; the dog, the hard rubber ball, the wind-gauge at the lighthouse on the jetty, the scratch on the thigh of the woman in the boat. Beckett situates each of the major scenes at the edge of water: the weir, the jetty in the storm, the boat pushing off the bank and eventually coming to rest in the flags. He juxtaposes the schematic division of the basic scene with the finely detailed description of these three locations. This evocation of an expansive world contrasts sharply with the 'ruinstrewn land' that Beckett's theatrical characters usually perceive, even in memory. One must remember, however, that the words voiced by this tape are not the manifestation of Krapp's present consciousness. Krapp's mind, as the principal image of the play, is no closer to the consciousness of the younger Krapp who speaks these words than is Vladimir to the mind of the young man who stood on the platform of the Eiffel Tower fifty years earlier. Even though the older Krapp performs actions which are identical to those reported by the younger voice, the play represents the gap between the two voices more than the identification of one with the other. While in the earlier plays Beckett juxtaposes past and present, the past itself has no authentic presence; it exists only as residue – worn objects and equally worn stories, diminished in their use and repetition. In this way Beckett distances the past from the consciousness of the characters even as they handle the objects and speak the stories.

In *Krapp's Last Tape* Beckett marks that division scenically with the physical separation of the character and the stories he tells. We have no sense that the consciousness of the old Krapp encompasses and assimilates these memories with much greater comprehension than Clov recalls his arrival at the shelter. Something, of course, draws Krapp to the story of the woman in the boat, and he plays that section of the tape three times. However, we do not know if he is responding to the memory itself or to his memory of earlier playings of the tape. The old Krapp is puzzled by the noun *equinox*; he cannot remember the meaning of *viduity*, and searches a dictionary to discover the significance of the word used by the younger. While the past in *Krapp's Last Tape* seems to have more presence, authenticity and vitality than the remnants of the past in earlier plays, Beckett uses the physical or scenic division between character and memory – the separation of the figure of Krapp and the voice of the tapes – to diminish the immediacy of the past. The limited consciousness of the older listens to the more vital and fluent speech of the younger, but the degree to which he comprehends the significance of the words and marks their connection to actual events remains equivocal. As his lips move during the final playing of the episode in the boat, the audience recognises the possibility that he may mouth those words because frequent listening makes them familiar, not because they constitute a living image within his consciousness.

Character

In the trilogy the *persona* of the speaker frequently divides to conduct an internal argument with itself. The final moment of *The Unnamable* includes just such a division. One part of that troubled consciousness wants to halt, to lose himself in darkness and silence; the other voice within him urges him to continue: '. . . I can't go on, you must go on, I'll go on, you must say words, as long as there are any.'[5] This division of voices within the same speaker manifests the antithesis that marks each of Beckett's heroes: the impulsion to continue speech and, thus, existence; the desire for silence, and therefore, death.

Beckett uses this division in *Krapp's Last Tape*

schematically by dividing the character between the sixty-nine-year-old man and the recorded voice of this same figure thirty years earlier. The physical division allows the old man to listen to the words of the younger at will. The old Krapp becomes an *eiron* responding to the imposture of the pretentious younger *alazon*, and at several points the inflated rhetoric of the younger man stimulates the old man to respond with amused but self-deprecating laughter. Beckett compounds that scheme in skilful doubling. As the old man listens, the voice of the thirty-nine-year-old Krapp itself comments upon a tape recorded by him 'ten or twelve years ago', and the voice responds ironically to the resolutions made by the youth in his twenties:

> The voice! Jesus! And the aspirations! (*Brief laugh in which Krapp joins*) And the resolutions! (*Brief laugh in which Krapp joins*) To drink less, in particular! (*Brief laugh of Krapp alone*)

Here we see the old man, caught in the same habits of the very young Krapp, perceiving the irony of the thirty-nine-year-old speaking in ironic amusement at the naïveté of the man in his twenties. Beckett marks several points of identification between the older and the younger Krapp, especially habits and routines, building an image in which the two *personae* merge and divide.

Despite the correspondence between the two Krapps, the younger voice reports an experience that the older finds distant and strange as well as familiar. The memories on the tape, the three incidents, provide the central material of the play, and we hear them with the image of the partially deaf, older Krapp bent over the machine, letting the voice of his younger self play in his consciousness. Two of the memories report the dissolution of relationships: the first records the death of his mother, balanced by the slighter incident of his rejection by the young nurse. The third incident takes place as he sails in a punt with a young woman under blazing sunlight. This moment records their agreement to terminate the relationship: 'I said again I thought it was hopeless and no good going on, and she agreed, without opening her eyes.' The centre incident, the moment of recognition at the edge of the sea, assumes the form in this recorded 'retrospect' of a vision in which Krapp sees some kind of totality: 'suddenly I saw the whole thing. The vision, at last.'

> This I fancy is what I have chiefly to record this evening, against the day when my work will be done and perhaps no place left in my memory, warm or cold, for the miracle that . . . (*hesitates*) . . . for the fire that set it alight.

Krapp avoids this section of the tape deliberately. He impatiently winds the tape forward, passing over the statement of the vision which, the voice announces, replaced the belief that he had been 'going on all . . . [his] life'. Our only indication of the nature of that vision comes in the next section which he inadvertently plays next: ' . . . clear to me at last that the dark I have always struggled to keep under is in reality my most –'. Beckett's characters frequently confront two different forms of darkness: the external darkness, the potential condition of the world that Clov will find if he leaves the shelter, and the internal darkness, the silence in which the self no longer attempts to affirm its being in speech and no longer seeks to imagine itself as an object in some lighted arena. Krapp does not want to hear this segment of the recording. Beckett keeps his motive hidden. While this moment may have been an

1. *En Attendant Godot* at the Theatre de Babylone, Paris in 1953, with Jean Martin and Roger Blin.

2. *Waiting for Godot* at the Royal Court Theatre, London in 1964, with Nicol Williamson and Alfred Lynch.

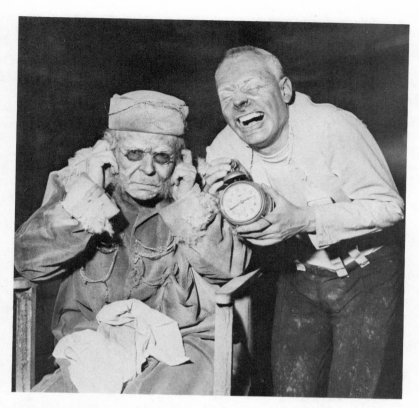

3. *Fin de Partie* at the Studio Champs Elysees, Paris in 1957, with Roger Blin and Jean Martin.

4. *Endgame* at the Cherry Lane Theatre, New York in 1958, with Lester Rawlins and Alun Epstein.

5. *Endgame* at the Cherry Lane Theatre, New York in 1958. P. J. Kelly as Nagg.

6. *Play* at the Old Vic Theatre, London in 1964. Billie Whitelaw, Robert Stephens, Rosemary Harris.

7. *Krapp's Last Tape* at the Forum Theatre, New York 1972. Hume Cronyn as Krapp.

8. *Happy Days* at the Royal Court Theatre, London 1974. Peter Hall directing Peggy Ashcroft.

9. *Happy Days* at the Royal Court Theatre, London 1979. Billie Whitelaw.

10. *Rockaby* at the Centre for Theatre Research in Buffalo, New York in 1981. Billie Whitelaw.

epiphany for the younger Krapp, the significance of the revelation has diminished in the mind of the older. This undisclosed miracle induced the 'fire that set it alight', and this is probably the same fire that burns in him at the end of the tape when he dismisses the value of the earlier years and the relationships that they included. This tape, perhaps, marks the beginning of Krapp's isolation – or, if not beginning – its primary confirmation. Krapp's insistence upon returning to the memory of the young woman in the boat and his avoidance of the vision scene may suggest that one aspect of his consciousness denies the validity of that choice.

In the tape he records for his sixty-ninth birthday, Krapp develops an image of himself in isolation, venturing forth into the outside world with no significant encounters. His memory of attending vespers, when he fell asleep and fell out of the pew, probably triggers his recurrent singing of 'Now the Day Is Over', an image which supports the sense that this event is an ending. At this point he is still tied to his sexual relationship with women, recounting the incidents with Fanny, the 'Bony old ghost of a whore'. In this last tape, as well, he refers indirectly to the woman recalled by re-reading the novel *Effie* (*Briest*): 'Could have been happy with her, up there on the Baltic, and the pines, and the dunes.' Once again Beckett situates Krapp's memory on some side near the water. Beckett doesn't allow Krapp to sustain this idyll, however, and he questions the possibility that this relationship would have been happy for him and, as well, questions his own ability to make her happy: 'Could I? (*Pause*) And she? (*Pause*) Pah!'

The repetition of images of dissolved sexual relationships, in combination with the physical image of the isolated Krapp, represents time in a scheme that is typical of Beckett: the graphic realisation of a single moment that appears to be the manifestation of an extended but unrevealed history. The characters in Beckett's plays confront the evidence of the past and recognise the distance between the time that evidence represents and the present. Beckett does not reveal Krapp's motive for choosing this particular tape; that purpose remains one of the unarticulated determinants that keep us from supplying the narrative history that Beckett does not provide. The tape, however, marking the death of his mother and the termination of an important sexual relationship, expresses a conflict between an acute desire to be free of relationship and a keen desire to be accepted – to be *seen* – by another. We need write no history for Krapp because that opposition of desires, subject to the processes of time, constitutes a sufficiently dramatic image of character itself.

6
'Embers' and 'Happy Days'

After the première production of *Krapp's Last Tape* Beckett resumed his practice of writing in French with the novel *Comment c'est*, which he began in December 1958. He returned to drama and English, however, with *Embers*, a radio play that was produced by the BBC in 1959.[1] As Krapp reviews images of the eyes of his sexual partners, the old man demonstrates the acute need to be perceived by others. In *Embers* Henry creates imaginary listeners to perceive his continuous discourse, and Beckett concentrates upon this single figure who summons the voices of others to reconstruct the past.

'Embers'

Time
Each of Beckett's plays prior to *Embers* focuses upon an

event: the rendezvous to meet Godot, the departure of Clov, Dan Rooney's birthday and the day of the railway accident, and Krapp's sixty-ninth birthday and the occasion of his 'last' tape. No such unique distinction marks Henry's walk along the sea. This day seems typical, not extraordinary. Whereas Beckett subtly stresses the typicality of the days represented in the earlier plays, he makes them occasions of potential significance. The text of *Embers* has no need of that occasion.

Like *Krapp's Last Tape*, *Embers* assembles a group of fragments from its hero's biography and presents them outside the context of an inclusive narrative. These fragments, arranged achronologically, present the image of a life of failed relationships: Henry suffers the pain of being seen as a failure, a 'washout', by his father who went into the sea immediately after this condemnation in a suicidal final swim; Henry marries Ada, and after years of 'hammering away at it' they produce an unpleasant child, Addie; the relationship between father and daughter is unsatisfying, and the relationship between husband and wife grows difficult and estranged – an estrangement compounded by Henry's obsessive need to isolate himself within the private bounds of his invented conversations. Beckett moves freely among the temporal segments of that narrative, using his freedom from the physical constraints of theatrical space to reveal broad leaps in Henry's consciousness from one moment in time to another.

Henry's perception of his father – his identification of his likeness to and difference from this figure – dominates the first moments of the drama as he evokes his father's presence and attempts to establish some kind of communication with him. When that effort fails as, by implication, it has always failed, he begins to tell an old story of his own invention, the unfinished tale of Bolton and Holloway. This narrative concerns a physician's late-night visit to an old friend who has called him to perform some act. Holloway, the doctor, finds his friend in a darkened room, lit only by the embers of a failing fire. Bolton, old and troubled, pleads with his friend. Holloway clearly knows the object of his friend's begging, but Beckett leaves the nature of the request unspecified. Holloway refuses to perform the act, which seems abhorrent and dangerous to him personally. Critics have speculated on the nature of Bolton's plea, a request he has made before, and it may be that Bolton is asking his friend and physician to release him from suffering through euthanasia. Henry continues his story but interrupts it to report his final conversation with his father in which he refused to go out for a swim with him and received his father's final condemnation before the old man committed suicide. He then moves into a brief reference to his wife, an unpleasant episode with his daughter, punctuated by her wail. He discusses the banality of his wife's conversation and suddenly she is there, sitting next to him on the shingle. This conversation, which occurs within the location of the basic scene, appears to take place in the present, but Ada does not really move into the scene physically, and certain clues show that this dialogue actually took place years before when their marriage was only twenty years old and Addie was still a child. Henry returns then, in memory, to the past of their courtship. This memory is interrupted by a comic scene between the child and her music teacher, an episode followed by a similar evocation of her session with a riding master. In a subtle transition, Henry next moves from hearing Ada recite a series of negative instructions – 'Don't stand there thinking about it. . . . Don't stand there staring. . . . Don't wet your good boots' – into the woman's imploring series of *don'ts* as he first made love to her in a secluded hole within the shingle near the present scene.

As Henry continues to reconstruct this dialogue with Ada she recounts her meeting with his father. She leaves, and Henry improvises upon her story, attempting to build it into a more complex and extended narrative, but he fails and returns to Bolton and Holloway, ending that recitation with: '. . . ghastly scene, old men, great trouble, no good. (*Pause*) No good. (*Pause*) Christ!' He then reviews his almost empty agenda for the evening and the next two days, noting only the plumber at nine: 'Nothing, all day nothing.' The play ends, as it began, with the sound of the sea.

Scene

Embers begins with the 'scarcely audible' sound of the sea; this subtle opening establishes the scenic location. Next the listener hears the sound of Henry's boots 'on shingle'. In this by-play between the sea and the noise of the character on the stony shoreline, the playwright places his protagonist, as yet unnamed, into a scenic space within a few economical seconds. The recurrent sound of the sea maintains the sense of place in *Embers*, keeping the character, as the listener conceives of him, in that specific scene throughout the performance. Each of the succeeding sounds and characters arise from within Henry's consciousness. The only sound external to his mind is the sound of the sea itself and the noise his movement makes along the shingle.

The first figure Henry entertains in thought is the silent presence of his father. 'My father, back from the dead, to be with me. . . . simply back from the dead to be with me, in this strange place.' Henry tells his character within his mind where they are: 'That sound you hear is the sea.' Next Henry summons the presence of his wife, Ada. The listener should recognise that both of these secondary characters are not present within the physical scene because while Beckett represents the sound of Henry's movement along the shingle, these figures slip in and out silently.

> HENRY: . . . Are you going to sit down beside me?
> ADA: Yes. (*No sound as she sits*) Like that? (*Pause*) Or do you prefer like that?

In *Embers* the past presents itself to Henry through other voices. These voices, however, have no presence apart from his consciousness.

The sea presents an antithetical image to Henry. He must stay near it, and yet he attempts to distance himself from its sound. He hears the noise, the 'sucking' of the waves along the shore continually, and he maintains a constant conversation with others and with himself to cover that noise. He reports his attempt to flee from the sea on a trip to Switzerland and the futility of that flight:

> Today it's calm, but I often hear it above in the house and walking the roads and start talking, oh just loud enough to drown it, nobody notices. (*Pause*) But I'd be talking now no matter where I was, I once went to Switzerland to get away from the cursed thing and never stopped all the time I was there. (*Pause*) I usen't to need anyone, just to myself, stories . . . .

In *Waiting for Godot* Estragon marks the presence of 'dead voices' within his consciousness that 'talk about their lives'. Vladimir and Estragon deliberately create verbal and physical activity to avoid the sound of those voices within their minds. Henry opens his mind to the 'dead voices' that Gogo and Didi ignore. Initially his stories constitute a strategy to avoid the sound of the ocean – the place his father loved and chose for his suicide. These invented stories suffice, and Henry can provide his own audience. Then he needs the presence of others to form an ostensible audience. Eventually he invokes the imaginary audience within his mind and peoples it with those who knew him in his early years as his stories and invented conversations revert to the past.

The sequence of speech and sounds in *Embers* creates the physical scene of the strip of shingle along the shore. In the course of the play the listener learns that this space is a bay or estuary with land on two sides. The smaller space within that scene is Henry's consciousness itself. Here – in this image of a character's mind – spaces, scenes, characters and events are distributed according to an associative pattern, achronologically. Whereas the repetitious sound of the sea notes a literal time, the rhythm of the waves moving according to the temporal laws of tide, the inner space contains a sequence that is atemporal, suspending time, out of synchronisation with the omnipresent and yet relentlessly progressive image of the sea.

Character

Ada's description of Henry's father 'sitting on a rock looking out to sea' establishes a physical image that characterises Henry himself:

I never forgot his posture. And yet it was a common one. You used to have it sometimes. Perhaps just the stillness, as if he had been turned to stone.

114

Henry's demand that she continue this recitation – 'Keep on, keep on! (*Imploringly*) Keep it going, Ada, every syllable is a second gained' – relates him to the writer-protagonists of the novels, using their speech/writing to fill the moments until death.

Henry, like his predecessors in Beckett, is an old man, approaching death, but he seems to have been engaged in the process of dying since he was a young man. His ambivalent feelings towards the sea, his need for its presence and his compulsive desire to drown out its sound, seem to manifest the typical Beckett antithesis: the desire for death and the desire to keep its threat at bay by continued speech. The sea, the place of his father's suicide, functions as a constant reminder of death in a clear but subtle associative pattern; the playwright puts language – the speech of memory and invention – in opposition to the sound of the sea.

Henry reflects the basic conflict in his invented story, the narrative of Bolton and Holloway. Bolton, placed strategically between the room and the dead white stillness of the winter exterior as he parts the velvet hangings and stares out of the window, allows the fire to die and the room to become completely dark. Holloway, uncomfortable in the cold and dark, rejects his plea and keeps him alive and suffering. Henry's story is like the other tales told by Beckett's characters that either displace their present situation into some fiction or, at least, connect obliquely to their present life. Henry uses this narrative to avoid an explication of the failure of his relationship with his father, but the connection is unclear and remains indeterminate, providing a gap in the narrative. In the middle of his recitation Henry focuses on the silence of this invented world and modulates from his recognition of this silence into the sound of a drip –

reminiscent of Hamm's 'There is something dripping in my head', a remark that Nagg, Hamm's father, ridicules. At this point in Henry's story, he stops and calls for his father, but, like Hamm at the close of *Endgame*, he receives no answer.

'Happy Days'

Samuel Beckett began writing *Happy Days* in its original English version in early October 1960. The dating of the drafts show that he completed the new play on 14 May 1961. Alan Schneider directed the première production which opened at the Cherry Lane Theatre in New York on 17 September 1961.[2] Ruth White played Winnie, the garrulous middle-aged woman, half-buried in the strange mound of earth that fills the stage. In *Happy Days* Beckett develops his convention of representing a single figure in space, but Winnie's acute need to be seen and heard, a need that corresponds to Henry's demand for an imaginary listener, makes the actual presence of Willie necessary. Consequently, she performs for the equivocal audience of her almost mute husband. At one point in the first act Winnie attempts to understand why Willie does not respond and she voices this telling statement:

> One does not appear to be asking a great deal, indeed at times it would seem hardly possible – (*voice breaks, falls to a murmur*) – to ask less – of a fellow-creature – to put it mildly – whereas actually – when you think about it – look into your heart – see the other – what he needs – peace – to be left in peace – then perhaps the moon – all this time – asking for the moon.

Her rationalisation of Willie's indifference voices her own desire for freedom – for isolation, silence, darkness.

Time

The idea of a *day* provides Samuel Beckett with a measurement of activity that fits his sense of dramatic form. Day seems to be the only unit of time that Vladimir and Estragon can comprehend, and Beckett divides their experience into a series of days, each similar but each a discrete unit. The tramps separate at night and reunite when the light of the day exposes them to each other's view. Hamm and Clov also separate at night, and the single act of *Endgame* represents a day in Hamm's life, beginning with the act of Clov uncovering him to begin their interaction. The association between daylight and the experience of being seen works subtly in *Godot* and *Endgame*, but in *Krapp's Last Tape* and *Happy Days* the intensely lighted stage space clearly functions as an arena in which the protagonists confront themselves self-consciously. In both plays the concept of night and darkness promises relief from the compelling need to create an image of the self.

Beckett works here within the same scheme in which Racine framed the concept of *le jour* in *Phèdre*. I point out this example of classicism in Beckett for two reasons: firstly, we tend to think of Beckett's dramatic writing as wholly innovative, springing up in full realisation, independent of dramatic or theatrical tradition. This is a false idea that derives from the shock of his radical simplification of conventions. Secondly, this particular relationship between Racine and Beckett illustrates Beckett's ability to penetrate an apparently restrictive or arbitrary formalism and, consciously or unconsciously, to exploit it. The unit, day, provides the temporal boundaries of classical drama, and the conventional period of time in which the dramatised action should occur. While this unifying principle does operate in classical tragedy, with

117

some exceptions, its limits become more stringent in seventeenth-century French drama. In Racine's *Phèdre*, *le jour* works both as a temporal unit and as the designation of a public space, illuminated by the daylight, in which the heroine's nature is exposed, both to the court and to herself. Phèdre feels compelled to dress herself in regal garments and to reveal herself to public view, and yet when she enters that open space, strongly lit by the sun, the light unnerves her:

My eyes are dazzled by the daylight that I see again,
And my trembling knees give way underneath me.

Oenone reminds her:

You wanted to present yourself and see the light again.
You see it, Madame; and now you are ready to
hide yourself
From the daylight you have come to seek.

These brief citations from I.iii of Racine's tragedy illustrate Phèdre's antithetical motives: her desire to reveal herself in the light and her acute fear of that exposure. She moves into the day that represents both the segment of time which encloses her catastrophe and the space in which her guilt is made public.

Beckett also uses the opposition of day and night, light and darkness, to signify the antithesis between private and public. I do not assert that Racine's notion of day is a specific source. My suggestion is simpler: that Beckett's familiarity with neo-classical drama, particularly Racine, revealed to him the potential significance of this concept as a means of building an image of space and time. Phèdre's words clarify that she perceives the lighted public arena as the space in which she imagines herself, that public site stimulates her self-conscious awareness of herself. In *Happy Days* Winnie uses the temporal and spatial notion of the day as the basis of her perception of herself.

Winnie, caught in her mound of 'scorched earth', is subject to unending 'Blazing light' in what seems to be an endless noon. A piercing bell rings periodically, dividing segments of time into arbitrary days and nights. She believes herself compelled to separate her activities according to the bell for waking and the bell for sleep. In a version of *Happy Days* that precedes the published text, the bell is an alarm clock controlled by Winnie, but in the final text the bell is sounded by some external agent who marks the time and Winnie senses its hostility: 'The bell. (*Pause*) It hurts like a knife. (*Pause*) A gouge. (*Pause*) One cannot ignore it.'

Within the limits of the bell's division of day and night, Winnie is free to organise her day at will. Consequently she confronts the basic problem of allocating her activities in such a way that they are distributed throughout the day so that she is not left with 'hours still to run, before the bell for sleep, and nothing more to say, nothing more to do . . . .' While Winnie is caught in a situation in which she must improvise the events of her day, as Vladimir and Estragon are forced to do, she has the resources of a multitude of objects at her disposal in combination with a sense of time that encompasses the idea of a past in which these objects played meaningful roles.

Winnie's perception of these objects connects her to the memories of specific days and important incidents within them. She focuses on five particular days, three of them associated with her relationship to Willie. The first two memories appear to be prior to her life with Willie: the childhood memory of sitting on the lap of Charlie Hunter whose death Willie has just announced in his periodic reading of the yellowed newspaper with which he fills his days. This memory, which may be either a recollection of a childhood experience or an early erotic encounter, stimulates her memory of her first ball, her second ball, and her first kiss with a 'Mr Johnson or Johnston, or . . . John*stone*' in a toolshed. Specific objects stimulate the memories tied to Willie, and she identifies each of these incidents as 'that day'. The first comes as she inspects a strand of her hair:

> Golden you called it, that day, when the last guest was gone – (*hand up in gesture of raising a glass*) – to your golden . . . may it never . . . (*voice breaks*) . . . may it never . . . (*Hand down. Head down. Pause. Low*) That day. (*Pause. Do.*) What day?

She marks the next specific day early in the second act. Here she remains caught in the earth, sunk to her neck, incapable of using her arms. The bag remains at her side, and she speaks to Willie: 'The bag is there, Willie, as good as ever, the one you gave me that day . . . to go to market. (*Pause. Eyes front*) That day. (*Pause*) What day? The parasol lying beside her triggers her memory of the next specific day, a recollection of a summer outing which is reminiscent of Krapp's memory of the woman in the boat: 'The sun shade you gave me . . . that day . . . (*pause*) . . . that day . . . the lake . . . the reeds. (*Eyes front. Pause*) What day?' Close to the end of the second act Winnie returns to her memory of the day of the party and her encounter with Willie alone after the guests had gone:

> That day. (*Pause*) The pink fizz. (*Pause*) The flute glasses. (*Pause*) The last guest gone. (*Pause*) The last

bumper with the bodies nearly touching. (*Pause*) The
look. (*Long pause*) What day? (*Long pause*) What look?

Beckett organises each of these references to a specific
day within a similar pattern. The memory is stimulated by
a specific object, or as in the second reference to the party,
the memory includes a tangible object and the action
associated with it. While she is able to discuss these
incidents from the past in detail, Winnie cannot hold on to
them or place them within a context. Each of these
passages ends with a pause followed by the desperate
question 'What day?' Winnie's consciousness divides
between her attempt to encompass the past and her clear
recognition that the past has no reality, no substance in her
consciousness apart from the words that describe it. She
perceives that her world suffers change and radical
deterioration, but that once she has moved from one state
to another the reality of the earlier moment is annihilated.

Then . . . now . . . what difficulties here, for the mind.
(*Pause*) To have been always what I am – and so
changed from what I was. (*Pause*) I am the one, I say the
one, then the other. (*Pause*) Now the one, then the
other. (*Pause*) There is so little one can say, one says it
all. (*Pause*) All one can. (*Pause*) And no truth in it
anywhere.

At certain moments her fiction of happiness fails, and
Winnie recognises that she cannot hold the past – the series
of exceptional days she mentions – she can only speak
about it.

She uses a simple time scheme – the opposition of the
present mode of existence to the 'old style', 'the sweet old
style'. She experiences the present through that scheme,

marking the differences between the past and the present and sustaining the practices and the stories of the 'old style' in this strange existence she leads at the moment. At specific times, however, she recognises that such differentiation is arbitrary:

> . . . did I ever know a temperate time? (*Pause*) No. (*Pause*) I speak of temperate times and torrid times, they are empty words. . . . And should one day the earth cover my breasts, then I shall never have seen my breasts, no one ever seen my breasts.

Winnie wavers between her recognition that her existence is dependent upon sustained speech and her realisation that language is self-reflexive, marking no real connection to the world it seeks to describe. Her awareness of the impossibility of knowledge is too painful for her to deal with except momentarily, and she returns to the fiction her speech maintains:

> My arms. (*Pause*) My breasts. (*Pause*) What arms? (*Pause*) What breasts? (*Pause*) Willie. (*Pause*) What Willie? (*Sudden vehement affirmation*) My Willie! (*Eyes right, calling*) Willie! (*Pause. Louder*) Willie! (*Pause. Eyes front*) Ah well, not to know, not to know for sure, great mercy, all I ask.

All Winnie needs to sustain her routine is the possibility that Willie still lives. She needs the potential audience that possibility constitutes. Comforted by her sense that he may live because she does not know for certain that he is dead, she is free to return to the process of voicing memories: 'Ah yes, . . . then . . . now . . . beechen green . . . this . . . Charlie . . . kisses . . . this . . . all that . . . deep trouble for the mind. (*Pause*) But it does not trouble mine. (*Smile*) Not now. (*Smile broader*) No no.' Throughout the text of *Happy Days* there are momentary breaks in which Winnie confronts the impossibility of differentiating between then and now, but she dismisses that recognition and pursues her disguise even though that fictional role itself attenuates and weakens.

In *Happy Days* Beckett returns to the two-act structure he used in *Godot*. As in *Godot*, we have no evidence that the second day of *Happy Days* follows the first immediately. As Winnie's consciousness functions in the second act, the time represented by the first act seems no more immediate to her than the memories she voiced then. That time when she had the use of her arms seems no less distant than her memory of the encounter with Willie after the party. For Winnie the past is irredeemable and is present to consciousness only in the words in which it is discussed; and she recognises that there is no truth within those words.

Scene

Beckett makes no attempt to explain the strangeness of Winnie's situation. Her memories suggest that she has not always been confined in this mound of earth, and her twice-repeated story of the man and woman who, passing by, speculate as to why she is there and why Willie does not dig her out, indicate that Winnie's experience is exceptional even within the fictional world of the play. Beckett leaves the cause of Winnie's confinement as indeterminate as the cause of the devastation that precedes *Endgame* or the motive that brings Vladimir and Estragon to their appointment on the barren plain of *Godot*. Beckett's dramaturgy does not include an examination of causality. While his characters seem possessed by specific images of the past, they do not examine their memory to seek an understanding of their present situation. That situation is a given, and memory – the text that revolves through their minds – envisages another time, another place, but does not establish a connection between that time and place and this moment, this space. Winnie's situation is, indeed, strange, but – as she herself says – '. . . here all is strange.' Beckett's description of the site is, as always, both simple and precise:

> Expanse of scorched grass rising centre to low mound. Gentle slopes down to front and either side of stage. Back an abrupter fall to stage level. Maximum simplicity and symmetry.
> Blazing light.
> Very pompier-trompe-l'oeil backcloth to represent unbroken plain and sky receding to meet in far distance. Imbedded up to above her waist in exact centre of mound, WINNIE.

Winnie suffers a hellish light that does not shift into darkness. She seems suspended at a point of infinite noon. While the mound of earth that holds Winnie captive provides a strong visual image of both her immobility and her isolation, the unchanging, relentless light which blazes down on her constitutes the dominant quality of this space. The mound functions to hold her in place in that light, preventing her from seeking the darkness of shade.

In *Waiting for Godot* Estragon anticipates the coming darkness with enthusiasm because it offers him the peace which comes when he no longer has to sustain the activity of waiting. However, for Winnie darkness remains a dream, and she frames that idealised reality in images of release from the light and from her body: '. . . why then just close the eyes – (*she does so*) – and wait for the day to come – (*opens eyes*) – the happy day to come when flesh melts at so many degrees and the night of the moon has so many hundred hours.' At this point, which comes in the first third of the play, the spectator recognises the hollowness of Winnie's affirmation of her present existence, the falsity of her repeated declaration that this day is a 'happy day', another 'happy day'. The real 'happy day' in Winnie's mind would be an extended night in which she would be free from the compulsion of creating a sense of a day and a sense of herself as the focus of her own perception. As long as she is caught within the blazing sunlight, she is tied to language and to the objects that language names.

The objects that surround Beckett's protagonists appear to be fragile and elusive, and his characters perceive them as the few remaining items in a world that suffers progressive depletion and exhaustion. These things provide the evidence of an earlier time in which they existed in their original state, accompanied by a plentitude of other objects. They hold no intrinsic symbolic or iconographic value. Their significance derives from their use by the characters. They exist to be spoken of, or – perhaps more accurately – they exist because they are spoken of. Consider the presentation of landscape and objects here at the beginning of Fizzle 5:

Closed place. All needed to be known for say is known. There is nothing but what is said. Beyond what is said there is nothing.[3]

The landscape of *Happy Days* embodies this image; nothing within it has significance apart from Winnie's speech. To sustain existence and a sense of herself within a

125

world she must continue speaking, naming those objects that she finds available and reaching toward the ephemeral images of the past they invoke.

The objects we see on the stage of Beckett's plays have a paradoxical existence. They are autonomous entities, and the consciousness of these characters can never possess them nor even be certain of their existence. These things have no significance, no functional or symbolic value apart from that assigned to them by the character. Because of their autonomy they remain both familiar and alien to the character who eventually recognises that the mental processes of identifying, naming and describing them is, ultimately, an arbitrary exercise of language. The distance between the object and the word that attempts to capture its presence remains incapable of being bridged. Beckett dramatises that irredeemable gap as he juxtaposes the tangible thing itself and the evanescent image of it held in the consciousness of the character.

In Beckett's plays other human beings are present to the protagonist only as objects; persons and things share a vulnerability to time because, as images in the consciousness of the protagonist, they are subject to the fluctuations of the mind that creates their significance as images. Beckett's discussion of Proust clarifies his sense of the relationship between consciousness and the object of its desire. This critical analysis, which Beckett wrote in 1929, defines models of the imagination that Beckett himself has employed in his writing. Beckett examines Proust's creatures as victims of time as he discusses the relationship between the perceiving subject and the object of its attention:

We are not merely more weary because of yesterday, we are other, no longer what we were before the calamity of

126

yesterday. . . . The aspirations of yesterday were valid for yesterday's ego, not for today's. We are disappointed at the nullity of what we are pleased to call attainment. But what is attainment? The identification of the subject with the object of his desire. The subject has died – and perhaps many times – on the way.[4]

Here Beckett posits a model in which the principal transition in time takes place in the subject, not the object. The perceiving and desiring consciousness, in these terms, is inconstant. Because the subject shifts and transforms itself in time, the object that was once desired is now seen as alien. The object appears to change in the process of becoming something else to the consciousness that perceives it. Keeping in mind that the dynamics of change are located within the perceiving consciousness that mediates its image of the object, consider Beckett's comment on the shifting value of human relations in Proust's writing: 'The object evolves, and by the time the conclusion – if any – is reached it is already out of date.'[5]

In the plays Beckett concentrates upon a single moment in time, and he is, therefore, unable to represent the complex transitions in the consciousness as it moves from moment to moment, losing its identity and reconstituting itself as some other being with other desires. Within the co-ordinates of the single moment, however, Beckett reveals Winnie caught within a structure formed by superannuated objects. Winnie's consciousness is divided: whereas one part of her mind envisages that happy day when death will release her from the earth, her objects and her relationship to these 'old things', her desire to maintain her life ties her to these objects because she needs them to sustain her conversation. She needs to process them in her mind in order to sustain consciousness.

Samuel Beckett

Character

Winnie is Beckett's most extended dramatic image of character. She maintains a veritable monologue for two complete acts, interrupted only briefly by the few terse comments of Willie. I have seen *Happy Days* performed many times, including Beckett's production of the play with Billie Whitelaw at the Royal Court Theatre in 1979. I have seen Winnie played by actresses with little experience and by actresses, such as the great Madeleine Renaud, who brought brilliance and virtuosity to the role. My experiences with this play in a variety of productions, including two which I directed, have forced me to recognise the temptation to perceive its principal character through the conventional schemes of realism. The indeterminacies of *Endgame* periodically frustrate our tendency to identify with its characters; and while we respond to the acute images of pain and suffering which Beckett represents in Hamm and Clov, our minds are consistently active during the performance, attempting to place these specific moments into a coherent narrative framework. Our belief in the emotional reality of these characters may be intense at certain moments, but that belief cannot be sustained sufficiently to bridge the discomforting ironies that mark the performance. Audiences, however, accept the peculiar given circumstances of Winnie's situation early in the performance, dismiss that disjunctive image and concentrate upon the personality of the woman. Spectators both admire her determination to endure and sympathise with her painful awareness of the physical and psychological damage time inflicts.

In *Happy Days* Beckett sustains the image of Winnie without the kind of interruption that the self-conscious references to the theatre make in both of the earlier full-length plays. However, our understanding of the irrelevance of the early debate about the identity of Godot should keep us from attempting to fit the characterisation of Winnie into a realistic structure that would attempt to explain her situation and predict her future. As we watch a performance of *Happy Days*, we should not imagine a biography for this woman; we should not invent a history of her marriage or attempt to determine the reasons for her confinement. We should, rather, concentrate upon the nature of her present dilemma only as the co-ordinates of the play itself define it. The lack of a coherent historical context provided a problem for many in *Godot*'s early audience and kept them from attending to specific images that were present in the performance. An experienced audience, we now know what to expect when we read or see a play by Samuel Beckett. The absence of context in combination with the specificity of images have become themselves a convention, and we expect to see a work within a form that joins an idiosyncratic situation with characters performing activities outside the framework of a narrative structure.

Because of the reduction of narrative incident and the strangely barren environments in which Beckett places his characters, critics and spectators have identified his plays as abstract. In the analysis of painting the adjective abstract is used in a very general sense to distinguish between the representation of objects and the use of painting to create an object itself, one whose design does not refer the observer to some artifact, person or place. Beckett's theatre is antithetical to abstraction in this sense. While his scenic environments are often bare and never refer to specific sites, his characters use these places in detailed and recognisable actions. Winnie, for example, lives in her mound as if it were a normal room within a bourgeois house. She attempts to approximate the regular procedures of life while captured in that site. At specific moments in Beckett's plays a spectator can witness a wholly understandable interaction between a character and a physical object. The character's perception, identification, use and response to that object build a highly concentrated dramatic moment that, outside the context of the play as a whole, could be seen as a keenly naturalistic imitation of life. For example, Winnie's frustrated yet persistent efforts to read the indistinct printing on her toothbrush, interrupted as her mind focuses on other things, provide a graphic portrait of a typical human act, and the individual spectator may affirm that typicality as well as identify with her specific feelings of frustration, persistence and triumph in success. Each of Beckett's plays constitutes a collection of such precise moments, moments in which he represents the character's consciousness in a struggle to perceive the world in which it finds itself. The plays, as complete structures, are not naturalistic, however, because Beckett does not place these specific moments within a historical context.

Dramatic realism calls for a belief in an idea of history, the concept of a movement through time that is directed by the interaction of many natural and cultural phenomena. The conventional structure of a realistic drama provides for the gradual but detailed revelation of the operation of those factors, an exposition of the progression of events that has brought the characters to this point in their history. That idea of history, of course, is irrelevant to the isolated segments of time that Beckett's drama represents. Beckett's characters exist in situations that are atemporal; and while the spaces they inhabit have been ravaged by time, they have no known history. The only past that exists is embodied in the words spoken by these characters, and these words produce disjointed, fragmented and ephemeral images. These images do not coalesce into a comprehensible sequence of events that explains the present situation. Beckett projects intensified images of human beings engaged in the minutiae of life but that intensity derives not from the exaggeration of these images but rather from the clarification produced by their isolation in bare space free from other reference.

Beckett's plays do not, therefore, call for a highly stylised form of acting. His roles demand that the actors performing them enact specific acts of perception and invest them with an imaginative belief in the reality of the object; then, as the character senses the autonomy of the object and the evanescence of his relationship to it, the actor has to be able to perceive the clear division between his consciousness and the object that cannot be encompassed or possessed. Actors trained in realism work most effectively in Beckett's plays, because they are accustomed to build a characterisation by establishing their belief in specific moments.

I have suggested that the speech of a typical Beckett character seems to divide into at least two different voices, each calling for a different world or perceiving a different reality. The division in Winnie's consciousness is clear but not as schematic as the division in *Krapp's Last Tape*. Winnie manifests antithetical desires. One of her voices sustains the fiction that this is, indeed, 'a happy day, another happy day'. However, the day that she creates within this fiction consists of the implementation of a sequence of routines that (1) have no relation to her present situation, (2) use objects that are themselves alien to the environment, (3) rely upon a combination of saying and doing in order to invest them with significance, and (4) appear to have become increasingly disconnected from

131

their original function. Her need to sustain the idea *day* in an environment in which there is no day, only an endless noon, compels her to enact these otherwise useless patterns of behaviour. She is trapped within a pattern of conventions that no longer have individual significance. Maintaining the fiction of a happy life does, indeed, sustain her image of herself as a civilised creature and keeps at bay the threat of the wilderness, that terrifying condition in which she would confront her absolute solitude and have no reason to continue speaking:

> Oh no doubt the time will come when before I can utter a word I must make sure you heard the one that went before and then no doubt another come another time when I must learn to talk to myself a thing I could never bear to do such wilderness.

The other half of the wilderness is the silence that comes from the freedom from all connection to the external world; in temporal terms it is 'that happy day to come when the flesh melts at so many hundred degrees and the night of the moon has so many hundred hours'. As long as Winnie is trapped in the earth, she seems forced to speak about her fiction of happiness. In Beckett's 1979 production of *Happy Days* at the Royal Court, Billie Whitelaw repeated the recurrent 'happy day' and its variants almost as an automaton, in radical contrast to Madeleine Renaud's virtuoso performance of an indefatigable optimist. Whitelaw's performance emphasised the hollow formalism of Winnie's routines and clarified the moments in which her despairing voice breaks the fiction of optimism.

A highly skilful actress can use *Happy Days* as a vehicle to exhibit a wide range of comic techniques. On the other hand, a more sensitive interpretation of the text reveals the division between Winnie's voices. The repetitive verbal units with which she sustains her fiction of optimism and vivifies her sense of the past constitute this play's version of the omnipresent text that revolves in the consciousness of each of Beckett's protagonists – the text that attaches itself to their imagination and repeats itself insistently. The despairing Winnie who longs for the peace, darkness and silence of death constitutes the primary voice of this character. The grim presence of that voice diminishes the brilliance of her secondary voice's fictitious optimism. For example, when Willie appears before her at the beginning of the final movement of the play, Winnie's response is ironic, not ebullient:

WINNIE: (*mondaine*) Well this is an unexpected pleasure! (*Pause*) Reminds me of the day you came whining for my hand. (*Pause*) I worship you, Winnie, be mine. (*He looks up*) Life a mockery without Win. (*She goes off into a giggle*) What a get up, you do look a sight! (*Giggles*) Where are the flowers? (*Pause*) That smile today. (*Willie sinks head*) What's that on your neck, an anthrax? (*Pause*) Want to watch that, Wille, before it gets a hold on you.

Her words to Willie are bitter and unpleasant, and she maintains that tone up to the point he speaks the single syllable 'Win'.

Win! (*Pause*) Oh this *is* a happy day, this will have been another happy day! (*Pause*) After all (*Pause*) So far.

The familiar 'So far' gives a subtle suggestion of the cynicism or despair that may underlie her declaration. At this point she begins to sing her song, 'The Merry Widow Waltz', and the play proceeds to its close.

Beckett leaves Willie's motive for his journey toward Winnie unclarified. He may, as some have noted, be attempting to retrieve Brownie, the revolver that Winnie claims he gave her to keep him from suicide. In any case, despite the tendency of audiences to read it so, the final moment in *Happy Days* is not an exercise in sentimentality. The tenderness and affection embodied in the cloying lyric written for Lehar's music is merely another of the banalities that Winnie voices in her effort to postpone facing the wilderness.

7
'Words and Music', 'Cascando', 'Play', 'Film' and 'Eh Joe'

Samuel Beckett has not written a full-length play since *Happy Days*. Instead he has produced a series of briefer dramatic works for stage, radio, film and television and, as well, a series of works of prose fiction. Whereas the shorter plays follow his typical pattern, representing images of the past revolving in the consciousness of his characters, they locate these figures in less specifically defined spaces. In fact, several of these shorter plays avoid conventional scenographic images altogether, using the stage or studio simply as a place that accommodates the characters' experience.

Soon after completing *Happy Days* Beckett wrote two radio dramas, the first in English for the BBC and the second in French for the ORTF.[1] The autograph manuscript of the first, *Words and Music*, shows that it

135

was written quickly in late November 1961.[2] John Beckett, his cousin, composed the music, and the play was broadcast in the autumn of the next year. The second, *Cascando*, represents a collaboration with Marcel Mihalovici, who had earlier composed an opera based upon *Krapp's Last Tape*. The composer was not able to complete the score promptly, and *Cascando*'s first performance was delayed until October 1963.

These two radio plays develop a structure upon which Beckett's later theatre works build, and they provide a clear transition between *Happy Days* and *Play*. *Words and Music* and *Cascando* juxtapose the past and the present in Beckett's typical scheme, but they use that structure to divide the functions of the writer's consciousness into the figure of a storyteller who creates fictions compulsively and a listening ego who judges them. In the earlier stage plays, where audiences perceive the individual characters as distinct persons, Beckett does not divide the psyche into fragments of characters, but in the closed verbal world of radio drama an individual consciousness can become the arena for action because a separate voice, as a unique thought or mental function, only maintains presence when it is being exercised. A sequence of discrete voices in a radio drama can represent the progression of images in consciousness more fluidly than three-dimensional figures in space in a theatre.

'Words and Music'

Character

In *Words and Music* Beckett provides three characters who seem to represent different psychic functions of a single consciousness: Croak, who is both authority and audience for whom the other two create and perform; Words, called

'Joe' by Croak, who supplies the narrative; and Music, called 'Bob' by Croak, a small orchestra which supplies music to accompany the narrative. Both Words and Music exercise a tendency to meet Croak's demands with clichéd responses. In the opening moments Words rehearses a rhetorical piece on Sloth, and when Croak informs him that the theme for this night is 'Love', he merely recites the piece he has been speaking, substituting the noun love for sloth. Two specific conflicts develop: first of all, neither Words nor Music are able to express themselves on the stated theme to Croak's satisfaction; and secondly, they are unable to reconcile the two media into a single, unified composition. After several false starts, however, they reach some kind of reconciliation on the second theme, 'Age'. Here Words touches upon the latent memory of a woman:

> Comes in the ashes
> Like in that old light
> The face in the ashes
> That old starlight
> On the earth again.

For the first time Croak directs his attention to the subject of the recitation rather than to its form. Music improvises a warm response to Croak's rapt attention in opposition to Words' insistence upon keeping the presentation cool. Croak shifts his attention back to formal concerns and demands reconciliation. Words then describes an erotic vision, focusing upon a woman's face as though bending over her in sexual embrace. She seems almost dead, 'were it not for the great white rise and fall of the breasts, spreading as they mount and then subsiding to their natural . . . aperture –.' After variations of this image

137

which represent the movement of the man's eyes down the body to the 'wellhead', Croak leaves and Words and Music are left to close alone.

In this text Beckett poses certain problematic relationships among a series of mental functions that come into play in the process of writing. *Words and Music* maintains the same kind of indeterminacy that is found in other works, but Beckett confronts them with a higher degree of self-consciousness here and in *Cascando*. While the storytelling function, the narrator *persona*, may be subservient to the ego that monitors it, this creative entity maintains an independent existence. Despite the fact that it may attempt to satisfy the ego's demands with formal, repetitious exercises, using words according to clichéd patterns, if forced, the storyteller shifts, experiments, probes and attempts to create something significant to this perceiving ego. This listener seems to have an acute need to hear the narrative; and yet, when that story touches upon some deeply personal memory, he cannot bear the experience and retreats in panic. At that moment when fiction seems to coincide with personal history, Croak responds in anguish: 'Lily!' As Words continues, he attempts to stop him, shouting an equally anguished 'No!' When the disobedient Words continues, Croak despairs, cries 'My Lord!' twice, drops his stick and leaves. Here Beckett explores the difficult relationship between fiction and autobiography. *Words and Music* may be an admission of the autobiographical nature of Beckett's writing, but if that is, indeed, the significance of this little drama, the recognition posits no simple relationship between personal history and writing. *Words and Music* does not provide the sense that fiction exorcises memory; on the contrary, as Words moves away from formulaic rhetoric and cliché into a form of writing that draws upon memory or, at least, coincides with memory, the ego that receives those images cannot accommodate the anguish they engender and moves quickly away from the narrative.

Scene

Before Beckett focuses upon the consciousness of his protagonist in *Embers* as the principal scene of the drama, he locates Henry in a physical situation. As the fragments of memory arise in Henry's mind, they can be organised into a truncated narrative sequence in the listener's imagination. No such original physical location or implied narrative sequence informs *Words and Music*. The basic perceiving ego, Croak, does not even begin the work. Words and Music provide the first 'presences'. Whereas these three characters represent functions of a single consciousness, Beckett does not integrate them into the image of a specific, whole person. Henry summons his memories, but Croak comes to them, exercises some control over them, and then leaves them, recognising that his control over them is arbitrary and limited and that they do not satisfy his need but, instead, produce pain. The arena in which *Words and Music* takes place is, quite simply, a space in which these functions can operate, come together and divide. The lack of a precisely defined scene depersonalises the text, but that distance – or coolness – may give Beckett the freedom to explore the autobiographical processes of his writing, the work of creating fictions that are, voluntarily or involuntarily, dependent upon personal memory.

Time

The temporal structure of *Words and Music* is simple. Beckett maintains a focus, as always, upon the immediate moment of consciousness as that mind perceives and mediates an image of the past. The description of the face in the fire and the woman in the field, images that put Croak into a state of anguish, provide the only suggestion of a past. Beckett provides no narrative context that would explain or justify Croak's reaction, but the integration of creation and memory makes this particular aesthetic project painful to him. Beckett seems to insist upon the importance of the past in the process of writing, and simultaneously, to express the desire to be free from the past.

'Cascando'

Cascando was originally entitled *Calando*, a musical term denoting a diminishing tone, but Beckett changed the title to *Cascando* when radio personnel pointed out to him that the original name might be confused with *calendos*, a slang expression for cheese.[3] Beckett then returned to the title of an early poem, *Cascando*, an Italian word meaning falling or stumbling. The manuscript of this play, dated from 1–13 December 1961, shows that Beckett began writing it almost immediately after completing *Words and Music*.[4]

Character

Whereas *Cascando* deals with the same division of functions as *Words and Music* – the directing ego, the narrator and music – the later radio play focuses more precisely on the difficulties encountered by the character of Voice, the narrating activity of this composite character. In *Words and Music* the storyteller maintains a distanced coolness; his autobiographical images bring pain to Croak, the ego receiving the narrative. In *Cascando*, Opener, the equivalent of Croak, maintains a less emotional attitude to the material Voice presents, but Voice himself suffers. His 'life' consists of a compulsive search for the right story; to find the right character and create the story that would earn silence and peace:

> VOICE: (*low, panting*) – story . . . if you could finish it
> . . . you could rest . . . you could sleep . . . not before
> . . . .

Voice's initial speech represents the process of writing fiction as a ceaseless and compulsive activity. Each work, in turn, becomes a failure as it is judged inadequate in comparison with the ideal narrative that will end the storytelling function. In that sense, each story becomes an exercise in preparation for the ultimate creation which, in Voice's concept of experience, will end time. That objective, apparently as unrealised and unrealisable as the objects of Tantalus' desire, sustains life, but life as tedious and joyless activity.

Beckett identifies that aspect of the self that perceives and judges the fiction-making as Opener, whose speech is *'dry as dust'*. This creature provides the occasion for the public presentation of Voice's activity. Unlike Words in the earlier radio play, who performs on demand, Voice speaks continually. Opener simply makes him audible or inaudible, and during those moments when he closes him, the listener misses the words he speaks. The continuity of the narrating voice during those periods when Opener closes it reinforces the division between the self-consciousness of the writer and that part of the psyche that supplies the stories he presents to the public. Voice remains enclosed in the process of telling his story, but Opener's speeches document the public nature of the writer's career: 'They say, It's in his head. It's not.'

141

What do I open?
They say, He opens nothing, he has nothing to open,
it's in his head.
They don't see me, they don't see what I do, they
don't see what I have, and they say, He opens nothing.

. . .

I don't answer any more.
I open and close.

Opener complains that *they* – the public or critics – claim
'That is not his life, he does not live on that.' However he
recognises:

I have lived on it . . . pretty long.
Long enough.
Listen.

At this point Beckett subtly integrates the three subjects of
the radio drama: the narrative of Woburn, Voice's attempt
to reach the ultimate story, Opener's public presentation
of the story. Opener declares that he has sustained his life,
in psychological terms, through the activity of his
fictionalising, and then he asserts that indeed he has
sustained that activity and his life 'Long enough'. His
desire to end compulsive storytelling coincides with Voice's
perception that he has reached his objective, the final
story.

Time

Voice's narrative tells the story of an ending typical of
Beckett: Woburn, an old man, leaves the shed he inhabits,
and in the night makes his way down a slope, through the
sand, to the stones, eventually going into the water, falling

continually – or, perhaps, throwing himself to the ground. He floats out to the open sea face down in an oarless, tillerless boat. Voice tells this story as if he follows the progress of Woburn with his own eyes. The event of the fiction is coextensive with the event of the narration. Unlike most of the stories that Beckett's people relate, this narrative seems to be spoken for the first time rather than being one version of a series of repetitions; and the fate of Woburn remains unknown to Voice as he follows the progress of the boat past the island towards the open sea.

The action dramatised in *Cascando* is the telling of the story. Beckett frames that action as two different experiences of the event of recitation: Voice's experience of reaching the objective he seeks, peace and silence, as he completes his final story; and Opener's satisfaction with the story he opens, a satisfaction that may mark the end of his process of making stories public. The suicide of Woburn – as a reflection of the consciousness of the storyteller (the composite of Voice, Opener and Music) – may be a displaced image of their movement into death. Beckett's works, however, enact the processes of dying; they do not imitate death.

The audience has no assurance, of course, that Woburn will die and that the tripartite narrator has completed his final story because Beckett ends *Cascando* in a combination of words and music as Voice focuses upon the drifting boat:

> . . . it's right . . . finish . . .
> ....
> no more stories . . . sleep . . . we're there . . . nearly . . .
> ....

just a few more . . . don't let go . . . Woburn . . . he

....

clings on . . . come on . . . come on –

....

(*Silence*)

The stage direction *'Silence'* may signify that Voice has reached his objective, but the words themselves establish no formal close to the narrative, leaving the ultimate end unresolved but potentially achieved.

Scene

The space implied in the radio performance of *Cascando* is almost the direct equivalent of the 'location' of *Words and Music.* Since the drama plays itself in the consciousness of the composite character, it demands no scenic designation other than a space in which the listening audience may imagine the three 'characters' fulfilling the functions they must perform. *Cascando* differs from *Words and Music* in that Opener self-consciously assumes that he is performing publicly. In that sense he places himself before an implicit audience as he opens and closes. Both radio plays assume the form of radio drama, using the facilities of a sound studio in the integration of narration and music. Before writing these two radio plays Beckett always gave his plays a scenic location and his characters reveal themselves, in part, through their perception and response to that specific space. Even though he refused to place these scenes in any geographical or historical context, Beckett did transform the bare stage of the theatre into a fictional environment. Even in *Embers*, as I have noted earlier, when he first uses the consciousness of a character as the scene, he carefully places that character into a scenic location at the beginning

144

of the drama. The non-space or functional space of *Words and Music* and *Cascando* marks a major transition.

'Play'

Beckett wrote *Play* originally in English, but the short piece had its first production in Ulm-Donau on 14 June 1963 as *Spiel.*[5] The première of *Play* in English took place in New York in January 1964, directed by Alan Schneider. In April George Devine produced *Play* in Britain under the auspices of the National Theatre. Rosemary Harris, Robert Stephens and Billie Whitelaw played the adulterous triangle. This performance introduced Beckett to Whitelaw's acting. Her vocal range and her sense of aesthetic discipline appealed to him immediately. Several years later, he wrote *Not I* for her voice just as he had written *Krapp's Last Tape* for the particular sound of Patrick Magee's speech.

Space

When Beckett returned to writing for the theatre after his work on *Words and Music* and *Cascando*, he used the space of the stage in a new way. The basic scene of *Cascando* is the space in which Beckett locates Opener, Voice and Music; the ostensible space and the actual space are identical – the sound studio. *Play* presents three human figures enclosed in urns, which the playwright places in no scenic location other than the stage itself. The light that plays on the faces of the two women and single man is, obviously, a theatrical spotlight. Like the sun that blazes down on Winnie and the lamp that hangs over Krapp's desk, this light initiates and sustains speech, but unlike *Happy Days* and *Krapp's Last Tape*, *Play* does not need a scenic justification for the light; it is simply there. The play represents three characters who are compelled to repeat their individual variations of a story of adultery, and the spotlight sustains that compulsion. The characters cannot perceive each other, and they are unaware of anything in their immediate environment other than the interrogating spotlight. The spotlight is not a symbol, but simply a theatrical mechanism that exposes the painful process of confronting the past. The urns hold the three characters in place, keeping them from escaping the light just as the mound of earth holds Winnie under the blazing sun. Winnie, however, explores the nature of her environment and questions it.

In the stage plays that precede *Play* Beckett's characters relate to the space they inhabit and the objects it contains, establishing clear phenomenological relationships to the scene in which the playwright places them. The three characters in the urns, however, do not use space in that way; they are conscious only of the darkness and the questioning light. Here Beckett takes another step away from the conventions of theatrical representation, exercising the freedom from specific scenographic space that he achieved in *Words and Music* and *Cascando*. The principal feature of the strange place that holds the urns is the spotlight that elicits speech. Beckett insists that this light must function within the space shared by the three characters: 'The source of light is single and must not be situated outside ideal space (stage) occupied by its victims.' The light which seeks these three characters, switching rapidly from one to another, provokes their revelations and speculations and, thereby, builds the narrative image as the audience arranges these atemporal fragments into a logical sequence. The light, which Beckett thinks of as a fourth character, perceives the presence of the three, but each of them is unaware of the other two, and do not recognise that the periods of darkness and silence they experience are filled by the voices of the others.

Time

The elimination of a conventional scene in *Play* derives from the fact that Beckett attempts here to diminish the sense of the immediate moment as a unique event in space and time. Each character tells a variant of a story of a triangular relationship: W1 senses that her husband (M) is having an affair with another woman (W2) and hires a private detective to follow him. The husband discovers the investigator and bribes him. However, the wife finds out the address of the other woman and confronts her. The husband, fearing that the wife will commit suicide, promises to give up the other woman. He continues to see W2, however, and the wife grieves. He confesses his adultery, promising fidelity once again. The wife visits W2 a second time, gloating over her success. The husband, in the anxiety of betraying both, leaves the wife and goes off with W2. Apparently he eventually leaves her, imagining that the two women have become friends, comforting each other.

Beckett breaks up the linear sequence of the narrative by giving each character a different rate of speed in their brief alternating units of exposition. Each character reviews the past chronologically, but the units do not align, so the spectator must shift and sort, building a coherent sequence as these fragments proceed. The wife moves quickly through her narrative so that the husband's explanation of his behaviour always follows her version. The basic temporal division is consistent with Beckett's earlier theatre, representing the tension between the immediate present, in which the character is caught in some kind of limbo, and his perception of the past which, like a fixed text, revolves through his mind repetitiously.

The moment the text represents constitutes one event of a series of interrogations. The two sections of *Play* encompass such events, the second an attenuated version of the first. The characters in *Play* have no sense of the immediate moment other than as an interrogation by the light. W1 maintains the keenest sense of self-consciousness, recognising that her action is an attempt to satisfy the light, to speak what the light desires so that she can earn continuous silence and darkness.

> Is it that I do not tell the truth, is that it, that some day somehow I may tell the truth at last then no more light at last, for the truth?
>
> . . .
>
> I can do nothing . . . for anybody . . . any more . . . thank God. So it must be something I have to say. How the mind works still!
>
> . . .
>
> But I have said all I can. All you let me. All I –
>
> . . .
>
> Is it something I should do with my face, other than utter. Weep?

Her sense that the light seeks some definitive version of the narrative or some final conclusive perception relates to the search that Voice describes in *Cascando* – his attempt to find the story that will end his compulsive storytelling. In the radio play Beckett suggests that Opener is the authority who has the power to determine if the story is, indeed, the one sought for, the one that will end speech. In *Play*, that judging ego becomes the light itself, opening and closing the speech of each of the three characters. Here Beckett posits no end, merely a series of repetitions, but in Beckett's Berlin production the intensity of the light wavered, growing dimmer and more tentative in the repetition, thereby suggesting that each future repetition may grow closer to the darkness for which W1 yearns.

Character

The plot of the implied narrative in *Play* concerns an adulterous triangle reminiscent of boulevard sex farce, but while Beckett maintains some of the humour and verbal wit, he removes *Play* from that genre by dehumanising and detheatricalising these figures. Each of these characters remains locked in a personal vision of the events, isolated in some personal torture. The complicated intrigues, deceptions, unmaskings and coincidental meetings that inform this kind of comedy do not form the substance of the action but merely shape each character's memory. The text that encloses the consciousness of the three figures assumes the clichéd language of bourgeois comedy. Almost each of Beckett's dramatic characters is encumbered by a verbal residue which remains fixed in consciousness, and the banality of the words that burden them constitutes an aspect of the grimness, not the comedy, of their situation. Beckett characterises them only in the words they repeat – the unpleasant shrewishness of the wife, the bizarre hysteria of the other woman, the insensitive and incompetent womanising of the husband. The 'toneless' delivery Beckett requests, however, suggests that innumerable repetitions of this material have robbed the words of any emotional content; the only feelings these characters maintain are directed to their present situation –

their victimisation by the light. W1's periodic plea, 'Get off me,' embodies an authentic emotion as does M's plaintive 'Am I as much as . . . being seen?'

Beckett's characters yearn for the confirmation of being seen by someone else; recall Winnie's plea: 'Could you see me, Willie, do you think, from where you are, if you were to raise your eyes in my direction?' Krapp returns three times to the memory of his younger self bending over the woman in the boat, putting her eyes in shadow so that she could open them and accept him within the compass of her vision. Simultaneously, Beckett's characters manifest an acute fear of being perceived by some unknown witness. The probing eye of *Play*, embodied in the interrogating spotlight, directs the rhythm of the entire performance. The interrogating light clarifies Beckett's use of the image of *being seen* and demonstrates the impossibility of separating the act of speaking from the image of the self as an object of perception. This theatrical device reveals more keenly than before the alignment of language and light in Beckett's dramatic vocabulary.

In Beckett's one filmscript, titled simply *Film*, he develops an image of a character whose primary motive consists of a desire to avoid being perceived.[6] In his introductory notes, Beckett writes:

Esse est percipi
All extraneous perception suppressed, animal, human, divine, self-perception maintains in being.

. . . . . .

Until end of film O is perceived by E from behind and at an angle not exceeding 45°. Convention: O enters *percipi* = experiences anguish of perceivedness, only when this angle exceeded.

Beckett wrote the basic text of *Film* in 1962, and Alan
Schneider directed the production in a filming session with
Beckett present in New York in 1964. This film shows a
fragile Buster Keaton hounded by the terrifying presence
of E. The short movie begins with O in the street,
positioning himself to avoid the pursuit of E's inquiring
eye. Keaton encounters an old couple coming toward him,
and when they enter the direct range of E's vision, their
faces register horror. O escapes to his tenement. In pursuit
E catches sight of a flower woman coming toward him,
and she collapses when she realises that E has seen her.
Closing himself in his room, O blocks out all possibilities
of being seen – putting out a dog and cat, masking a bird,
shielding a mirror, ripping down a print of the face of
God, even destroying the photographic images of himself
at various stages of life. Terrified, he recognises that E is
present with him in the enclosed room; and at the end of
Film, caught within his gaze, the camera reveals that E is,
actually, his own eye.

O half starts from chair, then stiffens, staring up at E.
Gradually that look. Cut to E, of whom this very first
image (face only, against ground of tattered wall). It is
O's face ... but with very different expression,
impossible to describe, neither severity nor benignity,
but rather acute *intentness.*

This shocking moment – perhaps the strongest single
point of recognition in Beckett – clarifies that the unseen
eyes that drive Vladimir into frenzied activity and puzzle
Winnie are their own. Within this particular scheme
Beckett suggests that the search for identity that compels
his characters to create themselves and maintain a dialogue
that sustains that creation is an attempt to shield

themselves from self-perception; that is, the identity maintained in activity and language constitutes a form of disguise and masks the self from its own perception.

In 1965 Beckett wrote a television script which seems to build on *Film. Eh Joe*, written for Jack MacGowran although it premièred on German television with a German actor, uses the figure of a man shielding himself from perception in a room similar to the space in *Film. Film* divides the protagonist into perceived and perceiver, exploiting the division between functions of consciousness that he worked out in the radio plays. *Eh Joe* builds upon that scheme, presenting a silent figure who responds to a voice which sounds within his consciousness.[7]

This female voice claims that Joe has often heard the voice of others in his mind. She speaks of Joe's relationship with some other young woman and narrates the story of this girl's suicide. Beckett refracts the narrative, removing it from its direct participants. Here again the action is not the incident narrated but recitation of the incident. Beckett presents the image of the past in the form of a text that the protagonist experiences as an alien presence within his consciousness. He does not summon the image; it plays involuntarily. The detailed description of the young woman's suicide presents an image of her eyes, after coitus, that relates to the image of the woman in the field in *Words and Music*: '. . . The pale eyes . . . The look they shed before . . . The way they opened after . . . Spirit made light . . . Wasn't that your description, Joe?'

Eh Joe is not one of Beckett's major dramatic works, but it is significant as a transitional piece. The division of a physical image of character and the voice that plays in mind furnishes a theatrical paradigm that Beckett continues to use and to develop productively.

8
'Not I', 'That Time' and 'Footfalls'

'Not I'

Beckett wrote *Not I* quickly. The original version is dated 20 March to 1 April 1972.[1] He intended the première performance to be at the Royal Court with Billie Whitelaw whose voice he thought he heard while writing the play, but circumstances intervened that caused Jessica Tandy to originate the role in a production directed by Alan Schneider at the Forum, a small theatre in New York's Lincoln Center. This performance was one event in a Beckett Festival that included *Happy Days* with Tandy and her husband, Hume Cronyn, and Cronyn in *Krapp's Last Tape* and *Act without Words I*. Under Beckett's close supervision Whitelaw performed *Not I* at the Royal Court in January 1973, in a double bill with *Krapp* (the protagonist played by Albert Finney).

Samuel Beckett made a clean break between the visual

presence of a character and the voice that revolves in that figure's consciousness in *Eh Joe*. When he next wrote for the stage, he pushed that scheme to as extreme a point as possible, reducing the image of character to an illuminated mouth in *Not I*. Like *Words and Music*, *Not I* embodies an important transition in Beckett's playwriting. His correspondence suggests that he recognises that he may have reduced the theatrical elements in *Not I* to the point at which it ceases to be a dramatic work. In a letter to a friend he writes: 'Thanks for your reactions to *Not I*. Encouraging to my hope that it may be theatre after all in spite of all.'[2] To discuss the nature of this major step in Beckett's process of simplifying and intensifying his theatrical images, I begin this discussion with the problematic image of character.

Character

Not I takes place in a black void. The audience sees an elevated red mouth, lit in sharp focus, with an almost imperceptible robed figure standing to one side. The rapidly talking mouth is speaking inaudibly as the house lights dim. Some time after the curtain rises and Mouth is illuminated, the words become audible: ' . . . out . . . into this world . . . this world . . . tiny little thing . . . before its time . . . in a godfor- . . . what? . . . girl? . . . yes. . . .' The text recited by this mouth tells the story, obliquely, of an old woman, almost seventy, who has suffered some kind of collapse while 'wandering in a field . . . looking aimlessly for cowslips'. As she returns to consciousness, according to the recitation, she perceives a buzzing in her head, accompanied by an intermittent light that bears some relationship to the noise. Eventually she realises that the sound consists of her words and that they are being spoken by her own mouth.

Mouth does not experience this revelation at the time of the performance; this recognition is merely one of several incidents reported in the text. The structure of *Not I* suggests that this performance consists of one recitation of a text that repeats itself endlessly in the consciousness that belongs to Mouth. *Beckett does not, however, provide any dramatic representation of that consciousness.* Mouth is neither metaphor nor metonym of the whole personality of a character. As the recitation discusses, the character perceives that text as a sequence of words that her mouth speaks involuntarily. The text lists biographical details and records incidents in the peculiar life of a character, but the only real characterisation of Mouth is the one created in the spectator's imagination by implication. Beckett limits the facts of that biography; they include a premature birth, unknown parents, an uneventful life moving from orphanage to old age.

Since *Godot* Beckett has attempted to remove the presence of his characters from the context of a coherent narrative. Although his characters are never young, the protagonists before *Not I* manifest an energetic commitment to the moment and an active engagement with the few objects that remain in their environment. In *Not I* he removes the source of that vitality by eliminating the character's awareness of both location and self. In earlier plays the spectator sees characters grappling with the words that repeat in their minds and struggle with their compulsive need to speak them. Even in *Play*, in which the characters are reduced to automatons as they recite their banal versions of the past, Beckett represents them in the immediacy of their conflict with the interrogating light that dominates their present. In *Not I* Beckett presents only the text; the consciousness that perceives it is absent, and the audience must not only create a sense of narrative through implication but construct an image of character as well.

In an early essay on Samuel Beckett, novelist Alain Robbe-Grillet discusses the techniques with which Beckett disintegrates the character of the heroes in the trilogy. He notes their progressive incapacity and their movement into small confining rooms – eventually into the jar that holds the trunk of Mahood, the protagonist of the third novel. Robbe-Grillet clearly identifies the challenge that theatre presented to Beckett. Here the author whose prose fiction attempts to dissolve the presence of his characters was faced with a medium whose use of living actors established images of human presence immediately and irrefutably:

> The condition of man, says Heidegger, is to be *there*. The theatre probably reproduces this situation more naturally than any of the other ways of representing reality. The essential thing about a character in a play is that he is 'on the scene': *there*.[3]

Robbe-Grillet discusses the ways in which Beckett works to diminish the presence of his dramatic characters, citing Hamm's declaration of his own absence and marking the instances in which this character substitutes storytelling and manipulation for the authentic presence he cannot achieve.

As Beckett continues to work in the theatre he refines the scheme that I have discussed repeatedly in this book: the juxtaposition of a verbal structure – a text, memory or sequence of recollected images – and a character who revolves that verbal structure in consciousness. In Beckett's scheme the past lays down layers of residue in consciousness, and the words that form this residue replace memory. Beckett dramatises consciousness by representing characters who self-consciously maintain an image of themselves as they imagine themselves to have been in the past, and, as well, an image of themselves as they exist in the present, keenly sensing the difference between the two. The most profound recognition these characters encounter in moments of acute self-awareness is the consciousness of their own diminishing presence. The character of Winnie is most authentically present to the audience when she suffers the sense of her imminent disappearance.

In *Not I* Beckett removes the image of the basic consciousness and presents only the text that repeats itself within it. These words embody no immediate awareness, no single act of immediate perception, only a sequence of images of events that occurred in the past. Beckett does not show that the consciousness of the character to whom Mouth belongs either listens to that recitation or has any sense of it. Beckett has succeeded in removing character from this dramatic performance. Of course, the absence of that perceiving consciousness initially puzzles and disturbs the audience; this dislocation causes them to focus intently on the elements of the work that remain: the words themselves. Here in the recitation that forms *Not I* Beckett represents an old woman who cannot claim her subjectivity and attempts to diminish her own image of herself by substituting the pronoun 'she' for 'I'. At those points at which she finds that substitution most difficult, she stimulates the physical response from the silent auditor who lifts his arms in a gesture which may indicate 'helpless compassion'. Even this sense of character, however, is communicated by implication.

Scene

The thought of speaking alone, becoming a voice crying in

the wilderness, terrifies Winnie. She needs the presence of Willie to give her an ostensible audience. The consciousness absent in *Not I* could not speak the 'I' that Winnie voices continually. The self-consciousness clearly evident in *Happy Days* when Winnie confronts the terror of absolute solitude has no means of expression in this later play. In Beckett's production of *Happy Days* at the Royal Court in 1979, as I have already noted, Billie Whitelaw spoke the recurrent 'happy day' refrain almost as an automaton, perhaps responding to the unwilled, automatic recitation of Mouth in *Not I* in which all that remains is the representation of involuntary speech. The principal feature of the scene of *Not I*, of course, is the illuminated mouth, elevated above the level of the stage. That image marks the absence of an image of character. The presence of the auditor contributes a suggestive image, but not a definitive one. He remains external and unrelated to Mouth, in no way completing the partial human image. This figure who responds physically, in decreasing strength, to those points in the text which struggle with the maintenance of the third person narrative, may be present to constitute the authenticity of the voice itself. Since there is no consciousness, no self-consciousness, to acknowledge its presence, the auditor is there to complete the cycle of speech and hearing.

Time

I know of no Beckett text in which the present has less immediacy. Even in *Play*, where Beckett has dehumanised his figures, the interrogating spotlight stimulates their pain and irritation. Although these characters seem frozen in their rhetorical mode, they maintain consciousness of the present moment. *Not I* provides a text that builds an image of the past, but in the performance of the play

Mouth's unconscious and automatic recitation of that text creates a sense of the absence of time. While the text holds internal temporal reference and builds a fragmented but cohesive history of the woman, Beckett provides no plausible occasion for its performance, neither a spatial nor a temporal context.

In the sixties and early seventies, actor-centred ensembles such as the Living Theatre and the Open Theatre created performance 'events' in which the immediate experience of both actors and spectators was primary. These groups attempted to establish situations in which the personalities of performers and audience would interact. A text, if used, functioned only as a scenario to stimulate the psychological exploration of the actor, and performers played themselves. Imitation or representation was, to the degree possible, abandoned in order to emphasise the immediate 'reality'. *Not I* aims towards the opposite. Here Beckett attempts to diminish the sense of immediate event, reducing the experience the audience encounters to a minimum, eliminating as far as possible the interaction between the actual *persona* of the actress playing Mouth and the audience. The actress does not imitate or represent a consciousness but, rather, the textual residue of a consciousness, the words a character once originated but no longer perceives. Nothing can come of this text; it cannot develop, extend itself, or grow more detailed; it can merely attenuate.

'That Time'

Beckett wrote *That Time* in the summer of 1974, and the play was performed at the Royal Court in the spring of 1976 to commemorate the playwright's seventieth birthday.[4] Patrick Magee, playing Hamm in the *Endgame*

159

mounted for the occasion, performed the old man of *That Time*. Beckett sees a clear relationship between *Not I* and *That Time*, categorising the latter as in 'the *Not I* family'. In this play he continues to experiment with the division between the fragmented events that form the implied narrative and the image of the character who has experienced them. Like the illuminated Mouth of *Not I*, the head of an old man, Listener, is suspended in a black void. Listener hears three separate recorded narratives, each originating from a different loudspeaker but each spoken in his own voice. Beckett divides the play into three segments. After the first few words of the first narrative Listener closes his eyes; after each voice has spoken four times, a 10-second silence marks the end of a movement, and Listener's eyes open, closing again when the second narrative sequence begins. Beckett repeats this division after the next twelve units, and after a final twelve the play ends. The final stage directions call for another 10-second silence, the eyes opening, and – half way through the silence, a smile.

Ruby Cohn describes Klaus Herm's performance of the final moment of the play in the production at the Schiller Theater Werkstatt that Walter Asmus directed in collaboration with Beckett:

Magnified in silence and strong white light, the head seems to pale and shrink under the rush of words in the dimmer light. Brightly illuminated at the last, his eyes glistening as though with tears, Herm's smile (not 'toothless for preference' as in the text) merged with his audible panting into a single scornful exhale-laugh – Beckett's last-minute inspiration.[5]

Listener's breath is audible before the voices begin, during the silences, and at the end of the play. The image of the face, however, remains still, provoking Beckett on occasion to question the play's suitability for theatrical performance.[6] In *That Time*, however, Beckett returns to the dramatic image of both speaking and perceiving consciousness. Reduced as the *persona* of Listener is, Beckett uses him as the image of a whole *character*, showing both the verbal residue of a failing mind *and* the being who suffers that failure.

Scene

Following the spatial scheme of *Not I*, Beckett eliminates the sense of a location in the scene of *That Time*. The play does not take *place* in any literal sense. The spatial division between face – perceiving consciousness – and voice marks a separation between psychic functions, allowing the audience to recognise that while these three individual strands of memory play in a regular pattern, they are not controlled by the consciousness that perceives them. These discrete narratives, which intersect subtly, revolve in Listener's mind, but the unifying patterns they form do not suggest Listener's organisation or assimilation of them. While they have more presence than the kind of residue represented by Mouth's text, they are not the exact counterpart of the self-conscious inventory of events that comprises the deliberate retrospection of some of the earlier characters. Consequently, the division of voice and face, establishing an arbitrary relationship between the consciousness that hears and the words that it speaks, forms an image of mental function not of space. Listener maintains no sense of present location because that awareness would be external to the event dramatised.

Time

Beckett's return to the image of a consciousness perceiving images within itself does not signal a difference between the sense of time in *That Time* and *Not I*. While the consciousness of Listener is present to hear the words, the audience has no assurance that this presence does anything other than receive the text. Certain images may cause him pain, but the sequences recited by the three voices do not constitute an experience, *per se*, for Listener other than the experience of hearing a series of familiar words which, at one time, perhaps, held significance for him. Consequently, the spectator's attention focuses upon the narrative content of the three strands and their interstices which in combination build an image of the past. However, when B confesses the possibility that his story of romance is a fiction, each of the voices becomes suspect:

> . . . harder and harder to believe you ever told anyone you loved them or anyone you till just one of those things you kept making up to keep the void out just another of those old tales to keep the void from pouring in on top of you the shroud . . . .

This confession concludes the first movement and puts each of the preceding narrative accounts in a state of equivocation. The breaks in *Not I* occur when the implied character of the old woman struggles to maintain the objective form of her narrative; in *That Time* the similar interruptions follow moments in which each of the voices confronts a moment of doubt, spatial, temporal or psychological confusion.

Beckett fragments the audience's perception of past time by the division into three narrative voices. Voice A tells of an incident in which, as an old man, Listener attempted to

162

return to the ruins of a tower, Foley's Folly, a significant
site of his childhood where he once hid during the night
keeping himself company by speaking in several voices.
The first words of this narrative strand suggest that this
particular journey or pilgrimage was the last of a series of
such visits: 'that time you went back that last time to look
was the ruin still there where you hid as a child . . . .' This
excursion, however, proves futile, and A abandons the
journey without realising his objective. B explores the
memory of a moment in which a man and woman sit on a
stone in the sun near a river or walk on the towpath,
maintaining a sense of alienation and isolation even in a
clearly sexual relationship. Beckett puts the couple at the
edge of a river, as in *Krapp's Last Tape*, but in this
romantic interval – which may be a fiction – the lovers
avoid the acceptance of each other. They never look at
each other, but remain side by side, forgoing look or
touch. Voice C describes a time closer to the present age of
Listener. In this series C tells of Listener seeking refuge
from a perpetual winter in a series of public spaces – the
Portrait Gallery, Public Library and Post Office. In the
museum C experiences a disturbing moment of recognition
when he stares at an old painting behind glass and sees the
reflected face of another. He wheels around to catch sight
of the person, but Beckett suggests that the terror he feels
is caused by his recognition of his own reflected image,
repeating the image of self-perception that closes *Film*. In
the Public Library he also experiences one of those
moments after which he was never the same: 'not a sound
only the old breath and the leaves turning and then
suddenly this dust the whole place suddenly full of
dust . . . .'

Each of the strands locates Listener on a stone: the stone
of the ruin and the stone steps at which the old man came

to rest when he aborted his pilgrimage; the stone on which the lovers sit; and the marble slab of the bench in the Portrait Gallery. Strands A and C share a phrase that refers to the death of Listener's mother – 'was your mother ah for God's sake all gone long ago'. These strands also share the long green overcoat that Listener inherited from his father, the inheritance shared by many of Beckett's old men. These subtle intersections work to unify the sequences in the spectators' imagination, building parallels as well as a temporal framework, but this sense of unity does not come through the character's assimilation of the analogies. Beckett reveals only Listener's presence not his perception of the images these voices speak.

In earlier plays Beckett grounds the present experience of his characters in the connections they make to the physical scene they inhabit. That immediacy separates them from the past they describe – a past that exists only as images, pale and evanescent in comparison to the tangible objects they handle. In the stage plays that follow *Words and Music* and *Cascando* he experiments with the possibility of a freedom from location equivalent to the freedom from specific scene he discovered in writing the radio dramas. Freedom from location allows a freedom from event. To dramatise an event demands locating it specifically within space and time in some sense even if that specification is no more precise than a barren plain and a series of afternoons. From the beginnings of his playwriting, Beckett diminishes the significance of the immediate event by denying its uniqueness: the implicit succession of afternoons in *Godot*; the possibility that *Endgame* is one of a sequence of performed 'endings'; the typicality of Krapp's anniversary recording; the succession of days in *Happy Days*. However, in these plays the characters play the repetition energetically because their sense of identity depends upon it. In the later works, while the basic ingredients remain the same, Beckett shifts the emphasis. The central focus moves from the character's struggle with the repetition to the repetition itself. If the character is present, as Listener in *That Time*, his relationship to the repetition remains equivocal. The character becomes scenic, a location to house the repetition and place the narration.

Character

Those who are familiar with the printed texts of Beckett's plays recognise the recurrent '(*Pause*)' that punctuates the speeches of each character. In *Not I* the text that Mouth speaks contains no pauses other than the four major breaks. Here Beckett uses ellipses to divide phrases, and his instructions to the actresses playing Mouth have consistently emphasised the need for speed. The narrative voices of *That Time* speak paragraphs unmarked by the familiar pause. Within the pauses of *Godot*, *Endgame* and *Happy Days*, strictly programmed by Beckett, the characters respond to the text they speak; and within each of these pauses the audience has the opportunity to observe the consciousness of the character struggling with his situation. Indeed, these pauses are moments of self-consciousness as the words the characters speak play again in their consciousness. When Beckett removes the presence of the self-conscious character in *Not I*, the need for the pauses ceases. In *That Time*, Listener is beyond the point of any self-conscious mediation of the past and, in any case, his self-consciousness does not direct the voices. Consequently, the recitation – not being the source of a self-conscious reflection – proceeds without interruption.

The fragmented stories in *That Time* present the evidence of a consciousness that, at one time, used them as either fact or fiction. They remain in Listener's consciousness at some level, but he does not animate them. If they can be synthesised into a coherent image of character, the character they represent does not exist, because, in Beckett's terms, the permutations and transformations of the subject have altered him, many times, on the course from B to A to C, if that, indeed, does mark the equivocal chronology of *That Time.*

'Footfalls'

Billie Whitelaw performed *Footfalls* in the spring 1976 season at the Royal Court Theatre as part of the playwright's seventieth-birthday celebration, the same event that presented the première production of *That Time.*[7] In this play Beckett returns to the practice of revealing the nature of a dramatic figure by representing the relationship between character and scene. May, the protagonist of *Footfalls*, performs two compulsive activities: she paces along a prescribed length of the stage, and she recites a strangely disconnected narrative. According to the dialogue between the middle-aged heroine and the off-stage voice of her dying mother, she walks along this uncarpeted stretch of flooring to gain some confirmation of her presence in that place.

Beckett's scenic demands in *Footfalls* call only for the site of May's pacing:

Strip: downstage, parallel with front, length nine steps, width one metre, a little off centre audience right.

In the stage directions Beckett diagrams the pattern of her steps, and the text presents her movement according to a strict pattern of pacing, turn, pacing. The off-stage voice of the mother suggests an adjacent room, and the narrative May speaks refers to a church where, ostensibly, at one time she paced in the aisle. The space in which Beckett constructs the immediate moment, however, is no more extensive than the metre demanded by the activities of pacing and recitation. May not only revolves at the end of the limited nine steps, she 'revolves it all', playing some familiar sequence of memories or inventions within her consciousness. Beckett's characters review a narrative or partial narrative that, as a text, a familiar sequence of words, *revolves* in the mind. May's mother asks her: 'Will you never have done? (*Pause*) Will you never have done . . . revolving it all? . . . It all. (*Pause*) In your poor mind!'

The brief exchange about the material that May repeats in consciousness introduces her extended recitation. Beckett signals this transition with a pause and darkness. When the lights return, the strip of flooring is more dimly lit than before because the emphasis moves from the immediate physical site – and the relationship between mother and daughter at that moment – to the recitation itself. May continues her pacing, but Beckett concentrates upon the words she speaks as she 'revolves it all'. In *Not I* and *That Time* the narrating voices do not use the first-person pronoun. Mouth avoids it, speaking always of 'she'. The three voices of *That Time* address the listening presence as 'you', using the second person. In *Footfalls* Beckett represents the actual shift in voice.

I walk here now. (*Pause*) Rather I come and stand. (*Pause*) At nightfall. (*Pause*) She fancies she is alone. (*Pause*) See how still she stands, how stark, with her face to the wall. (*Pause*) How outwardly unmoved . . . .

Beckett's character uses the indefinite pronoun to refer, it seems, to her perception of the nature of her life. The 'it' that revolves in May's mind, the narrative that begins in this house, shares the indefinite reference of Clov's 'Finished, it's finished, nearly finished, it must be nearly finished.' The shift into third-person narrative and the indefinite pronoun both work to objectify the text, making it into a separate entity that seems disconnected from personal history. In that sense the recitation becomes a verbal structure repeated in consciousnesss rather than a sequence of memories in spontaneous association; and the relationship between character and story becomes even more equivocal in *Footfalls* than it was in *Endgame*.

9
'A Piece of Monologue', 'Rockaby' and 'Ohio Impromptu'

'A Piece of Monologue'

In 1978 Martin Esslin asked Samuel Beckett for a work to include in an early issue of the newly revived *Kenyon Review*, and after his successful performance of Beckett's prose work, *The Lost Ones*, David Warrilow of the Mabou Mines requested that Beckett provide him with a work on death that he could perform. Beckett replied to both requests with *A Piece of Monologue*, a dramatic fragment that he revised for publication in the 1979 summer issue of *Kenyon Review*. Warrilow performed the short play in New York in the autumn of 1979 and at Stanford University in the early spring of 1980. This brief work, combining a stationary figure and a retrospective text, works within some of the same conventions as *That*

169

Time, but *A Piece of Monologue* situates Speaker within a scenic space, not the void of either *Not I* or *That Time*, although the scene shares some of the qualities of the non-scenic space of these plays.[1]

Scene

The scenic co-ordinates of the work are simple: a white-haired figure of an old man, dressed in a white nightgown and white socks, stands next to a standard lamp 'with a skull-size white globe'. The faintly diffused light illuminates only one other object, 'the white foot of a pallet bed' just visible at stage right. The old man, Speaker, does not move. He recites a monologue describing a nightly action that at one time, apparently, he performed periodically, perhaps within the same room that this theatrical space represents. The only action that unequivocally takes place here is the present recitation of the text. While this space represents that room, Speaker does not use it to impersonate the routine he describes. He manifests no awareness of his immediate environment.

This simple image, continuing Beckett's movement away from strong scenographic details and yet moving back to some specific representative details, provides a useful example of Beckett's later dramatic technique; and, at this point, I would like to examine the relationship between space and time in *A Piece of Monologue* as a way of discussing the relationship between Beckett's earlier work and his most recent dramatic writing.

Time

In the disciplined process of writing dramatic texts, in the experience of seeing them performed by highly skilful actors, and in the work of directing significant productions of his own plays, Beckett has developed a profound understanding of the communicative value of the dramatic images he uses. While his plays have become briefer and more cryptic through the years, this brevity and intensification do not reveal an increasingly esoteric and private theatrical imagination. On the contrary, they demonstrate Beckett's increasing faith in the communicative resources of the theatre. His specific images have become briefer and more compressed as he replaces his already limited exposition with single images and brief statements that convey the sense, if not the detail, of some extended experience. When I use the term cryptic, I do not mean symbolic in the sense that these images need to be translated or decoded. On the contrary, the spectator needs only to read them sensitively, carefully constructing models from the data they project. Because Beckett returns again and again to the same images, I could discuss them as self-referential. While his writing is self-conscious in that sense, it is more useful to look at specific images as formal schemes, organisational strategies with which he works as he consistently distils his material, aiming at the simplest version that can communicate the process dramatised. Each unit of time represented in the action is metonymic of a succession of temporal segments – the two days of *Godot*, for example; and each specific image is a metonym of a larger image as it signals, but does not reproduce, a unit of narrative information. These images do not signify something other than what they are; they are neither allegorical nor iconographic. These brief, condensed signifying units replace narrative exposition, and the process of reading or attending a Beckett play demands a careful consideration of each unit in terms of its individual substance and its relationship to each other unit.

The discussion of the absence of narrative in Beckett has

become a critical commonplace, and my insistence on the presence of an implied or embedded narrative in Beckett's plays has been an attempt to counter that common argument. When I use that term, however, I also intend to emphasise the gap between the present consciousness and the specific image that occupies it. That distance between consciousness and image represents an irredeemable gulf between past and present. The sense of time which that distance implies forms the framework of an attenuated and equivocal narrative. To illustrate this point and, simultaneously, to examine Beckett's process of simplification and intensification, I consider three images from *A Piece of Monologue*, comparing them with their counterparts in earlier plays.

Beckett begins this play with a typical pun: 'Birth was the death of him.' Recall the two images of birth astride a grave in *Godot*. Pozzo voices the first, using it to illustrate the brevity of life, and later Vladimir extends it, using the image to embody his perception of the life that constitutes his experience, numbed by habit:

Astride of a grave and a difficult birth. Down in the hole, lingeringly, the grave-digger puts on the forceps. We have time to grow old. The air is full of our cries. (*He listens*) But habit is a great deadener.

In *A Piece of Monologue* Beckett condenses this image of life as the process of dying into six simple words; and he communicates their importance to the protagonist of this play by showing his desire to hear himself speak them again: 'Birth was the death of him. Again. Birth was the death of him.' The elaboration of images in the earlier plays seems dynamically complex in comparison to the telegraphic presentation of images in the late plays. These recent texts contain abbreviated restatements of images that Beckett has used throughout his writing. While these plays appear to abandon many of the physical resources of theatrical production, they deliberately exploit the communicative power of a few, highly selected theatrical images, and they depend upon repetition, providing the audience with the opportunity to deal with the abbreviated material several times. These texts demand a keen eye – even though there is less to see – and an even keener ear.

A Piece of Monologue dramatises a brief moment of reflection in an old man's life, but Beckett's skilful manipulation of reference builds the sense of an extended implied narrative – not necessarily an accurate history of this figure, but a series of painful images that inhabit his consciousness. Within the first few lines Speaker establishes the notion of his life as a sequence of units, two-and-a-half billion seconds, and a succession of 30,000 nights. Within one voiced image, Speaker evokes a sense of tedium analogous to that suffered by Vladimir and Estragon as they wait through their sequence of afternoons or by Winnie in her interminable progression of days.

Two implied visual images inform this text. The first represents a condensed version of the painful scene in *Film* in which O looks through and then destroys a group of family photographs. Recall that in the earlier scene, O studies seven photographs of himself alone and with mother, fiancée and child. This visual sequence includes the old man's poignant gesture of touching the little girl's face with a trembling finger, reducing a potentially complex narrative to a briefly realised visual image. The picture of the old man, reviewing and destroying these images of the past, suggests a strongly willed effort to separate himself from his own image, as that image is shaped by those versions of it recorded in the photographs and, as well, by his relations to the three critical women. In *A Piece of Monologue* Beckett does not show that act, but in the recitation Speaker describes an analogous one indirectly. He notes the significance of discolorations on the wall of the room in which he performed his nocturnal vigil, remembering well that these marks are the traces of the photographs that were at one time pinned to the wall before he destroyed them. He identifies their subjects: 'There was father. That grey void. There mother. That other. There together, smiling. Wedding day. There all three. That grey blot.' Here, in a radically shortened form Beckett poses an image of a family triad that we encounter repeatedly in tragic drama – father, mother, son. In the simplicity of Speaker's text the narrative context of this version of the conventional triad remains unexpressed. However, in a few words Beckett reveals that this protagonist found it impossible to live with the pictures and gradually destroyed them. This unelaborated revelation suggests extending suffering in an unsuccessful attempt to exorcise the past.

Speaker returns three times to the image of a funeral. This description, charting the details of a single event, functions as a metonym for a series of funerals. As he outlines the events of his life in units at the beginning of the text, Speaker declares: 'Two and a half billion seconds. Hard to believe so few. From funeral to funeral. Funerals . . . he all but said of loved ones.' The specific image describes a grave:

Grey light. Rain pelting. Umbrellas round a grave. Seen from above. Streaming black canopies. Black ditch beneath. Rain bubbling in the black mud. Empty for the moment. That place beneath. Which . . . he all but said which loved one?

Speaker refrains from identifying the dead as 'loved ones' in a rhetorical pattern that corresponds to Mouth's refusal to name herself in *Not I.* His cinematographic vision of the funeral 'Seen from above' attempts to detach him from the image, constructing the image of a single moment at the graveside from an elevated view rather than from the perspective of one of those mourners holding umbrellas. This subtle sense of distance matches the paradigm, 'he all but said of loved ones'. Beckett manages, in a few words, to embody the conflict between the desire to return to painful memory and the attempt to objectify memory and, thereby, to neutralise it.

Here, reduced to a repetition of the text of his opaque recitation, Speaker has only speech, and within that text he returns to the time when he both spoke and performed his nightly sequence of actions:

> Stands staring beyond half fearing what he's saying. He? [This moment questions his pattern of identifying himself in the third person.] The words falling from his mouth. Making do with his mouth. Lights lamp as described. Backs away to edge of light and turns to face wall. Stares beyond into dark. Waits for first word always the same. It gathers in his mouth. Parts lips and thrusts tongue forward. Birth.

In the final repetition of these sentences he omits the word, 'Birth', that signals the next repetition of the recitation. This omission may suggest that this particular voicing of the words is the last.

Character

Beckett's *A Piece of Monologue* does not represent an old man groping through a painful series of memories but, rather, an old man repeating the words left in consciousness after that struggle, using the habitual recitation of these words to fill the time until death. The spectator realises that the recitation does not represent a freshly perceived vision of the past and is, instead, the manifestation of a habitual repetition, one of an extended series of repetitions that may, at this point, hold little significance for their speaker. In *Play* he begins to call for a toneless quality in the recitation of narrative incident. These figures come to life only in their response to the immediate threat of the interrogating spotlight. The toneless quality of Speaker's presentation in *A Piece of Monologue* demonstrates the emotional distance between the events described and the present condition of the character who recites.

'Rockaby'

Two recent plays have been produced at special festivals held in Beckett's honour at American universities. *Rockaby* was performed by Billie Whitelaw at the State University of New York at Buffalo on 8 April 1981, and *Ohio Impromptu* at Ohio State University in Columbus on 9 May 1981. Both productions were directed by Alan Schneider.[2]

Beckett continues to work in an increasingly simple physical framework. *Rockaby* divides its single character into a listener and her recorded voice; *Ohio Impromptu* presents two identical characters, one who reads and one who listens.

Scene

When Beckett stops exploring the immediate processes of his characters' consciousness and focuses instead upon the recitation of a text that plays in their mind, his need for strong scenographic images dissolves. Whereas in his earlier plays the characters are actively engaged in their relationship to the space they inhabit, in these later works his characters attend only to the words they hear. In *Rockaby* the only space required is the immediate location of W's rocking chair, her present station. Her renunciation of external reality is so complete that the room itself has no reality to her; her world is limited to the chair, and that single unit, in combination with light and darkness, forms Beckett's scene in *Rockaby*. The division of character and voice, of course, creates a spatial image, objectifying the figure the voice describes, This separation, as well, works to dramatise W's use of herself as 'her own other', a notion she resorts to when she abandons her search for another like herself.

Time

Rockaby contains four narrative sections, each initiated by W's command, 'More'. Since the first segment begins after this command, the audience should assume that the recitation is a continuation of a text rather than the beginning of a whole narration. In this simple way Beckett diminishes the sense of the performance as a unique event, suggesting that this recitation is a partial repetition of a series of retrospective voicings that occur in W's meditation.

The first section details W's decision to stop 'going to and fro' in the outside world in search of 'another like herself'. The recorded voice notes that it is *'time she stopped'*, and W joins V in speaking that phrase in reference to her quest in the outside world. The second segment repeats the decision to end that activity, rephrasing the action implied in section 1:

so in the end
close of a long day
went back in

This section marks that ending and, as well, describes the beginning of her next phase of activity – sitting at her upstairs window, searching the windows opposite to see another, 'one other living soul / at her window / gone in like herself'. Beckett begins this section with the ending of the first phase of activity rather than the beginning of this particular vigil, probably in order to emphasise the series of endings, each of which marks a reduction in the objective of her search. The third section jumps ahead to the end of the next and final phase of her search in which she limits her watch to a search for a raised blind that would suggest the presence of another creature. This section describes the ending of that vigil, using the repeated phrase 'till in the end / the day came' to specify the time when she decides to abandon this phase, that, once again, it is *'time she stopped'*. As before, W joins V in speaking these words. In the fourth section V describes W's movement downstairs to sit in her mother's rocking chair where she will wait for death. This section, therefore, introduces the audience to the time of the present moment; and the diminishing voice and the gradual decrease in movement as W rocks may indicate that this moment marks her death.

Beckett does not specify how long W has spent in each of the four phases of activity since V narrates the final day of phase 1 and phase 3, and the beginning of phase 2. Each of these transitional points seems to serve as a metonym for an extended series of days. V reports that W's mother spent years in her process of rocking as she waited until death. As usual Beckett focuses upon the penultimate portion of a life.

'A Piece of Monologue'

Character

Rockaby maintains the conventional division between the figure present on the stage and the voice that plays in the character's consciousness. While the interaction of different voices in one consciousness occurs in Beckett's earlier writing, this division between the listening ego and the narrating voice becomes a clear formal strategy in *Words and Music*, and Beckett gives it visual form in *Eh Joe*. For example, the division of monologue into an internal dialogue in the final section of *The Unnamable* anticipates the more schematic separation in the later plays: ' . . . you must go on, *I can't go on*, you must go on, *I'll go on*, you must say words, as long as there are any . . .' (italics mine). Even the subtle shifts in Hamm's transition from direct speech to performance as he plays his mock-heroic play-within-a-play work towards a division between speaker and listener in which Beckett represents a character assuming and then questioning an attitude, posture, belief or perception. The alternation of optimism and despair produces at least two different voices in *Happy Days*, and perceptive audiences can separate the compulsive speaker from the woman who longs for silence and peace. In *Happy Days* Winnie's commitment to language constitutes a bond as fixed as that which holds her in the earth. In *Not I* and *That Time* Beckett's protagonists no longer have the will to make that commitment; apparently the recitation revolves in their consciousness involuntarily. These characters experience speech – verbal or silent – rather than will it.

In *Rockaby* Beckett's heroine summons her diminishing inner voice to recite the story of her renunciation of a quest to find 'another creature like herself'. She wills her retrospection, initiating the playing of that voice with her command 'More', but her will weakens and she speaks

179

each of the repeated commands with a softer sound. The voice itself decreases in the final section, marking a gradual but progressive attenuation of its vitality. Beckett's description of W as 'prematurely old', suggests that her movement toward death is a willed renunciation rather than a physical failure. Her elaborate costume, a black sequined evening gown with fancy head-dress, marks both the uniqueness of the occasion of her retreat to the rocking chair and, as well, her re-enactment of her mother's action. Whatever her motive in wearing this dress, it constitutes the remnant of an earlier life. In *Happy Days*, Winnie's costume, her pearl necklace, her parasol, her bag and its contents, all suggest a more complex life in 'the old style'. In *Rockaby* Beckett reduces those signs of character and past time, distilling them into the suggestive images of the costume and the mother's chair. The voice clarifies that W perceives the retreat into the chair as a duplication of her mother's behaviour:

> right down
> into the old rocker
> mother rocker
> where mother sat
> all the years
> all in black
> best black
> sat and rocked
> rocked

Her movement into that specific place may signify any of a range of potential actions. The gesture may encompass her recognition that the perception of herself is the only possible objective, that she can only function as 'her own other'. The movement may represent her attempt to create herself within the image of her mother, structuring her present experience to duplicate her perception of her mother's experience. In this case, her renunciation of the world and the establishment of herself as 'her own other' actually avoids her own identity as she submerges it in her mother's image.

Beckett works here within a familiar dramatic scheme: the identification of the protagonist with a parent. For example, Orestes' mandate to revenge his father's murder encompasses the reinstatement of Agamemnon's political power as Orestes takes his father's place. Oedipus assumes his father's identity involuntarily, but he fulfils his role both politically and sexually. Hamlet sees himself compelled to behave in a role more typical of his aggressive father than himself. Phèdre envisions herself as the victim of the same curse that Venus imposed upon her mother. In the course of Ibsen's *Ghosts* Oswald grows into the likeness of his father, Captain Alving. In each of these cases, the protagonist's identification with the parent encompasses his or her destruction.

While it may seem that by comparing a simple reference in *Rockaby* to a series of parent/child relationships in dramatic literature I overload the significance of Beckett's image, I use this point to illustrate the communicative power of Beckett's unelaborated and ultimately indeterminate exposition. In each of these earlier plays, the child's likeness to and difference from the parent has defined his or her character; and, as these heroes assimilate the identity of the parent in a destructive course of action, they perceive that image, simultaneously, as a familiar and yet alien presence within their consciousness. In *Rockaby* Beckett suggests that antithesis with a minimum of contextual reference. As the spectator constructs the implied narrative, he may recognise that W's attempt to

181

seek 'another like herself' forms the opposite of her mother's solipsistic retreat. However, the text V speaks includes her recognition at three moments in the course of that search that it was *'time she stopped'*, and – at these points W joins V in speaking the phrase. These decisions may represent her conscious movement toward her mother's objective, that the abandonment or reconstitution of the search fulfils a predetermined pattern. Thereby, the mother's death provides a model that she elects to re-enact or, from another perspective, a restrictive limitation in which she is caught.

'Ohio Impromptu'

Retaining the division he initiated in *Words and Music*, in *Ohio Impromptu* Samuel Beckett differentiates between the storyteller and the authority who opens and closes that narrative activity. Beckett uses a simple but striking visual image to place his scene. The lights reveal two figures sitting at a table, both old men, both black-coated and white-haired. One reads from a book, and the other listens, directing the reader with his hand if he falters or stops.

Space

The division between reader and listener provides the primary spatial image. This separation of figure and voice, isolating the functions of speaking and listening, produces twin images in *Ohio Impromptu*: one who, apparently, initiates a retrospective act and the other who presents the words that constitute that memory. R reads a narrative that describes the recent history of an old man who grieves for the loss of a loved one. The old man moved from the place he shared with that person in order to 'obtain relief'.

He regrets leaving that place but, for some reason, cannot return to it. He experiences once again a special terror he felt as a young man in the darkness of the night. During one night a man appears to him and declares that he has been sent by this dear one to comfort him:

> Then drawing a worn volume from the pocket of his long black coat he sat and read till dawn. Then disappeared without a word.

The text suggests that the stranger repeats this routine periodically. Then, according to the book R reads, the man announces that the dear one has told him to stop his visits. R reads through to the end of his text, and the play ends by R reading and the two enacting the close of the narrative which states: 'No sound. So sat on as though turned to stone. The sad tale a last time told. (*Pause*) Nothing is left to tell.'

Throughout his plays Beckett works to differentiate narrative and character and, simultaneously, to place narrative (or the evidence of it) as an image within the consciousness of a character. That is, he does not, as Aristotle would demand, frame the character to embody an action. On the contrary, the report of the past assumes the form of a recitation or story that cannot be verified, that exists only as a text, memorised or written. If the image of the past is, indeed, a memory, its familiarity derives from the frequency with which it is spoken, not from the evocation of an actual event. Here, in *Ohio Impromptu*, what appears to be the description of the immediate past of the old man who listens takes the form of an actual text. The narrative is objectified for him and the audience in the presence of what it is, a text. The only connection between that text and the listener, L, comes in the spectator's identification of him with the old man in the story and in the identification of the reader, R, as the stranger who comes to him to read. In this play, therefore, Beckett removes the image of the past from the character who may have experienced it; and rather than speaking it (internally or externally), L hears it spoken by some external agent. The principal character opens and closes, performing the function of the perceiving ego in *Words and Music*. However the listener in *Ohio Impromptu* seems subject to the experience detailed in the text; he does not direct it.

Time

While Beckett's works do not establish a narrative context, they create a sense of narrative. The past is not organised into a coherent sequence in Beckett's plays because that type of structure would give the past an authenticity that would be inconsistent with his use of time. The implied narrative, revealed indirectly in fragments, presents a sense of experience suffered and then lost. Beckett reveals only enough detail about the past to establish a body of material sufficient to be questioned. That is, the implied narrative exists in order to be perceived as nothing more than image, inadequate memory or deliberate fiction. The narrative remains distinct from character in the form of a self-conscious reconstruction as in *Happy Days*, a mark against which the present deprivation can be measured as in *Endgame*, or as a series of images that revolve in the mind, possessing the consciousness, as in *Footfalls*. In *Ohio Impromptu* the identification of the listener and the protagonist of the narrative read to him is even more subtle. As the reader proceeds with the narrative that tells the story of the grieving man and his nocturnal visitor, the audience assumes that these two figures are identical with their fictional or textual counterparts. Beckett does not use the text in this play as a formal image, suggesting that the past in the mind forms a text which can be repeated on demand. The narrative, which the audience judges to be a description of L's immediate past, has presence as body of words. These words signal loss more than substance because their story reveals the absence of those persons and events to which they refer. The narrative, fixed in the text, cannot shift and vary, revivifying itself in adaptation and expansion, because the words are static. Since the powers of the perceiving consciousness can only deteriorate, this text will attenuate and diminish in time.

Scene

The development of Beckett's dramaturgy is analogous to the development of a single text within his canon, a careful process of removing the extraneous, condensing a few highly selected images, working toward the most economical use of the remaining textual and visual images. Another demand complicates this process of simplification: Beckett's need to question the authenticity of every presence the fiction evokes. As Robbe-Grillet points out in the provocative essay I cited earlier, the theatre is a medium of 'presences'. Consequently, to represent the epistemological question that is fundamental to his aesthetic Beckett establishes the presence of an image and, in the course of performance, diminishes that presence, revealing the fragility of its significance.

Beckett repeatedly presents characters who review images of the past; in fact, the voluntary or involuntary speaking of the past constitutes the immediate activity of almost every protagonist, but often these characters have no real awareness that the particular moment they enact has any significance that would distinguish it from a series of repetitions of the words they speak. Within these texts, which were created by them when they were more active intellectually and emotionally than they are at present, they recognise that the past they create may be an inauthentic version of actual events: '. . . just one of those things you kept making up to keep the void out . . .'. Even though Beckett avoids the realistic convention of establishing a coherent history for his characters, he establishes a sense of the past. While that past has no presence as cause, Beckett creates its immediacy in two specific processes: the present condition of the character shows the evidence of time and the space he inhabits contains the debris of an earlier time. These earlier moments, however, are beyond recall, beyond significance. The words that describe them constitute another kind of residue, but the reality they would signify has been lost. The narrative image in Beckett's texts must be perceived by their audiences so that they can, in the course of performance, question its authenticity as history.

When Solness climbs the tower in *The Master Builder*, Ibsen's hero recognises that the conceptual structures that he has used to envisage himself in reality have failed him. He deliberately substitutes the erotic fantasy of building 'castles in the air' with Hilde Wangel. He renounces the rational narrative, with its socio-economic justifications, that he once used to explain his behaviour just as earlier he dismissed the metaphysical interpretation of his vocation. He climbs the tower in a gesture of freedom from conventional morality, renouncing the validity of orthodox ethics and, at the same time, enacting his own punishment. Solness's apparent suicide signals the failure of his attempts to encompass reality within any number of schemes, and he exercises his will in the fantasy he shares with Hilde. W's renunciation of the external world in

186

Rockaby, or L's deliberate seclusion in *Ohio Impromptu*, as an image of modern consciousness is, surely, no more modern than that of Solness. Each of these protagonists rejects the possibility of comprehending reality. However, in Ibsen's play, the presence of that reality fills the stage in the concrete images of the external world. Consequently while the audience watching a performance of *The Master Builder* perceives the gap between that world and the consciousness of Ibsen's hero, the undeniable fact of that external world remains a strong presence. Ibsen, of course, helped to develop those conventions of realism that demanded the presence of authentic representations of perceived reality even though his protagonists could not assimilate that reality in their own efforts to conceptualise their experience.

The reality of the external world remains outside the text of *Ohio Impromptu*. The landscape the old man traverses has no existence apart from its image in the text read to him. In Beckett's earlier plays, audiences observe the characters responding to specific images of place and individual objects within these environments. Beckett clarifies, however, that the meaning they invest in those scenes and those objects derives from their use of them; the external world in which these characters exist has no intrinsic significance. These environments restrict the characters; as he progresses as a playwright, Beckett limits the physical activity of his characters, working toward the concentration upon mind and text that the immobility of his characters enforces.

While Beckett reduces the scene of his dramas to mind and text, he also progressively weakens the ability of that mind to perceive and respond to the words that revolve within it. The images that his earlier characters perceive are analogous to the shadows on the back wall of Plato's cave.

These characters differ from Plato's, however, in that they are aware that what they perceive is shadow. In their self-consciousness they recognise that they create the significance of these images as they use language to describe them. They are aware of the presence of the world that casts the shadow, but they have no means of perceiving it directly. In these later plays Beckett removes that sense of self-consciousness. The character no longer imagines himself as an object within some space. Beckett presents only the image of a diminishing consciousness and a text that plays for it. In the final plays the audience has no knowledge of how that mind responds to the text. The specific environments Beckett provides in *Godot* and *Endgame* stimulate their characters' speech, and they create at least the illusion of significance as they perceive and respond to these sites and the objects they contain. In *Rockaby* and *Ohio Impromptu* Beckett's protagonists no longer see themselves within space. The words with which they once identified their environments now rotate in the consciousness as the manifestation of habit, not perception.

References

1. Introduction

1. Samuel Beckett, *Cascando and Other Short Dramatic Pieces* (New York: Grove Press, n.d. [*Cascando* copyrighted, 1963]) p. 13.
2. Ruby Cohn, *Samuel Beckett: The Comic Gamut* (New Brunswick: Rutgers University Press, 1962) p. 95.
3. Samuel Beckett, *Murphy* (New York: Grove Press, 1957) pp. 249–50.

2. Waiting for Godot

1. Jean Anouilh, *Arts Spectacles* (27 February–5 March 1953) p. 1.
2. Martin Esslin, *The Theatre of the Absurd* (New York: Doubleday, 1961) p. 6.
3. Colin Duckworth, 'The Making of *Godot*', in Ruby Cohn (ed.), Casebook on *Waiting for Godot* (New York: Grove Press, 1967) p. 89. Duckworth and Fletcher cited in Deirdre Bair, *Samuel Beckett* (New York and London: Harcourt Brace Jovanovich, 1978), p. 381.
4. Samuel Beckett, *Molloy*, in *Three Novels by Samuel Beckett* (New York: Grove Press, 1965) p. 134.
5. Samuel Beckett, *Waiting for Godot* (New York: Grove Press, 1954) pp. 39b–40a. Further quotations from this play will not be noted individually.

189

6. Samuel Beckett, *The Unnamable*, in *Three Novels*, p. 302.
7. *Molloy*, p. 7.
8. *The Unnamable*, p. 294.
9. *Molloy*, p. 7.
10. Samuel Beckett, *Malone Dies*, in *Three Novels*, p. 180.
11. Charles R. Lyons, 'Beckett's Major Plays and the Trilogy', *Comparative Drama*, 5 (Winter, 1971–2) p. 261.
12. Anselm Atkins, 'A Note on the Structure of Lucky's Speech', *Modern Drama*, 9 (December 1966) p. 309.
13. See, for example, Walter H. Sokel, *The Writer in Extremis* (Stanford University Press, 1959) p. 39.
14. August Strindberg, 'The Author's Preface to *Miss Julie*', trans. Evert Sprinchorn, in Robert Corrigan (ed.), *Masterpieces of the Modern Scandinavian Theatre* (New York: Collier Books, 1967) pp. 140–1.
15. Cohn, *The Comic Gamut*, p. 211.
16. Ibid., p. 216.
17. William Empson, *Some Versions of Pastoral* (New York: New Directions, 1950) pp. 27–86.

3. Endgame

1. John Fletcher and John Spurling, *Beckett: A Study of His Plays* (New York: Hill & Wang, 1972) p. 132.
2. Samuel Beckett, *Fin de partie* (Paris: Les Editions de Minuit, 1957).
3. Samuel Beckett, *Endgame* (New York: Grove Press, 1958). All citations from the play will be taken from this edition and not noted individually.
4. Ruby Cohn, *Just Play; Beckett's Theater* (Princeton University Press, 1980) p. 174. See Richard L. Admussen, *The Samuel Beckett Manuscripts: A Study* (Boston: G. K. Hall, 1979) for a description of the manuscripts. Several years ago I made a detailed study of the material held by the Ohio State University Library, and my analysis of Beckett's work with the text builds upon that study. I have not seen the Reading manuscript and depend here upon Ruby Cohn's well-pointed description.
5. In the French text Beckett uses *finir* for Clov's opening speech and *casser* for Hamm's version. The parallel structure is obvious in the French text but not as striking as in the English translation.
6. Charles R. Lyons, 'Beckett's *Endgame*: An Anti-Myth of Creation', *Modern Drama*, 7 (Fall, 1964) pp. 204–9.
7. *Molloy*, p. 32.
8. I refer to the typescript of Beckett's translation of *Fin de partie* into English held at the Ohio State University Library.

References

9. Cohn, *Just Play*, p. 174.

10. Wolfgang Iser, *The Implied Reader: Patterns in Communication in Prose Fiction from Bunyan to Beckett* (Baltimore: Johns Hopkins University Press, 1974) p. 273. Iser's book was originally published as *Der Implizite Leser* (Munich: Wilhelm Fink, 1972).

4. All that Fall

1. Samuel Beckett, *All that Fall* in *Krapp's Last Tape and Other Dramatic Pieces* (New York: Grove Press, 1960) pp. 29–91.

2. This citation is from a manuscript version of the text of *All that Fall* identified as B in Admussen, held at the Humanities Research Center, The University of Texas, Austin, Texas.

3. Michael Haerdter, *Materialien zu Becketts 'Endspiel'* (Frankfurt: Suhrkamp, 1968) p. 88, cited in Cohn, *Just Play*, p. 230.

4. The *Fin de partie* manuscripts document this process well. See Admussen's discussion in the introduction to *The Samuel Beckett Manuscripts*, pp. 12–13.

5. Bair, p. 209.

6. Northrop Frye, 'The Road of Excess', in Bernice Slote (ed.), *Myth and Symbol: Critical Approaches and Applications* (Lincoln: University of Nebraska Press, 1963) pp. 7–8.

5. Krapp's Last Tape

1. Bair, p. 491; Admussen, pp. 61–2; Samuel Beckett, *Krapp's Last Tape and Other Dramatic Pieces* (New York: Grove Press, 1960).

2. Samuel Beckett, *Stories and Texts for Nothing* (New York: Grove Press, 1967) p. 111.

3. Samuel Beckett, 'Fizzle 8. For To End Yet Again', *Fizzles* (New York: Grove Press, 1976) pp. 60–1. Originally published in French as *Pour finir encore et autres foirades* (Paris: Les Editions de Minuit, 1976).

4. Rick Cluchey and Michael Haerdter, '*Krapp's Last Tape*: Production Report', in James Knowlson (ed.), *Samuel Beckett: Krapp's Last Tape, A Theatre Workbook* (London: Brutus Books, 1980) pp. 134, 143.

5. *The Unnamable*, p. 414.

6.   Embers and Happy Days

1. Samuel Beckett, *Comment c'est* (Paris: Les Editions de Minuit, 1961) trans. by the author as *How It Is* (New York: Grove Press, 1964). *Embers* is included in *Krapp's Last Tape and Other Dramatic Pieces*, pp. 99–121.

2. Admussen, pp. 55–6; Samuel Beckett, *Happy Days* (New York: Grove Press, 1961).

3. *Fizzles*, p. 37.

4. Samuel Beckett, *Proust* (New York: Grove Press, n.d.) p. 3. Originally published by Chatto & Windus, London, in 1931.

5. Ibid., p. 65.

7.   Words and Music, Cascando, Play, Film and Eh Joe

1. Both works are included in *Cascando and Other Short Dramatic Pieces* (New York: Grove Press, 1968) pp. 7–19, 21–32.

2. Admussen, p. 94.

3. Raymond Federman and John Fletcher, *Samuel Beckett: His Works and His Critics* (Berkeley: University of California Press, 1970) p. 70.

4. Admussen, p. 26.

5. *Play* is included in *Cascando and Other Short Dramatic Pieces*, pp. 43–63.

6. *Film* is also included in *Cascando and Other Short Dramatic Pieces*, pp. 73–89.

7. *Eh Joe* is also included in *Cascando and Other Short Dramatic Pieces*, pp. 33–41.

8.   Not I, That Time and Footfalls

1. Admussen, p. 72. *Not I* is included in *Ends and Odds: Eight New Dramatic Pieces* (New York: Grove Press, 1976) pp. 11–23.

2. Bair, p. 627.

3. Alain Robbe-Grillet, 'Samuel Beckett or "Presence" in the Theatre', in Martin Esslin (ed.), *Samuel Beckett: A Collection of Critical Essays* (Englewood Cliffs: Prentice Hall, 1965) p. 108.

4. *That Time* is included in *Ends and Odds*, pp. 25–37.

5. Cohn, *Just Play*, p. 269.

6. Ibid.

7. *Footfalls* is included in *Ends and Odds*, pp. 39–49.

9. A Piece of Monologue, Rockaby and Ohio Impromptu

1. *A Piece of Monologue* is included in *Rockaby and Other Short Pieces* (New York: Grove Press, 1981) pp. 67–79.
2. *Rockaby* and *Ohio Impromptu* in *Rockaby and Other Short Pieces*, pp. 7–23, 25–35.

Bibliography

Books

Admussen, Richard L., *The Samuel Beckett Manuscripts: A Study* (Boston: G. K. Hall, 1979). This is basically a reference work, but it presents a clear picture of Beckett's process of composition, and documents whenever possible the real chronology of the works.

Bair, Deirdre, *Samuel Beckett* (New York: Harcourt Brace Jovanovich, 1978). Bair has written the only full-length biography of Beckett, and her work contains a great deal of interesting material. This work should be read with care, however, and with constant reference to footnotes so that the reader can see the kind of evidence upon which any particular speculation is based.

The following critical studies should be helpful to readers who wish to gain a clearer understanding of Beckett's work and his place in twentieth-century fiction and drama.

Cohn, Ruby, *Samuel Beckett: The Comic Gamut* (New Brunswick: Rutgers University Press, 1962).

—————, *Back to Beckett* (Princeton University Press, 1973).

—————, *Just Play: Beckett's Theater* (Princeton University Press, 1980).

Fletcher, John, *The Novels of Samuel Beckett* (London: Chatto & Windus, 1964).

Bibliography

Fletcher, John and Spurling, John, *Beckett: A Study of His Plays* (New York: Hill & Wang, 1972).

Hoffman, Frederick J., *Samuel Beckett: The Language of the Self* (Carbondale and Edwardsville: Southern Illinois University Press, 1962).

Chapters in Books

Bersani, Leo, 'Beckett and the End of Literature', in *Balzac to Beckett: Center and Circumference in French Fiction*, (New York: Oxford University Press, 1970).

Esslin, Martin, 'A Theatre of Stasis – Beckett's Late Plays', in *Mediations: Essays on Brecht, Beckett, and the Media* (Baton Rouge: Louisiana State University Press, 1980).

————, 'Samuel Beckett: The Search for the Self', in *The Theatre of the Absurd* (Garden City: Doubleday, 1969). This is a revised edition of the original published in 1961.

Iser, Wolfgang, 'When Is the End Not the End? The Idea of Fiction in Beckett', in *The Implied Reader: Patterns of Communication in Prose Fiction from Bunyan to Beckett* (Baltimore: Johns Hopkins University Press, 1974).

Perloff, Marjorie, ' "The Space of a Door": Beckett and the Poetry of Absence', in *The Poetics of Indeterminacy: Rimbaud to Cage* (Princeton University Press, 1981).

Index

Index

Index

Index

OTHER GROVE PRESS DRAMA AND THEATER PAPERBACKS

17016-X ARDEN, JOHN / Plays: One (Serjeant Musgave's Dance, The Workhouse Donkey, Armstrong's Last Goodnight) / $4.95

17208-6 BECKETT, SAMUEL / Endgame / $2.95

17233-7 BECKETT, SAMUEL / Happy Days / $2.95

17204-3 BECKETT, SAMUEL / Waiting for Godot / $3.50

17112-8 BRECHT, BERTOLT / Galileo / $2.95

17472-0 BRECHT, BERTOLT / The Threepenny Opera / $2.45

17226-4 IONESCO, EUGENE / Rhinoceros and Other Plays (The Leader, The Future Is in Eggs, or It Takes All Sorts to Make a World) / $4.95

17016-4 MAMET, DAVID / American Buffalo / $3.95

17040-7 MAMET, DAVID / A Life in the Theatre / $6.95

17043-1 MAMET, DAVID / Sexual Perversity in Chicago and The Duck Variations / $3.95

17092-X ODETS, CLIFFORD / Six Plays (Waiting for Lefty; Awake and Sing; Golden Boy; Rocket to the Moon; Till the Day I Die; Paradise Lost) / $7.95

17001-6 ORTON, JOE / The Complete Plays (The Ruffian on the Stair, The Good and Faithful Servant, The Erpingham Camp, Funeral Games, Loot, What the Butler Saw, Entertaining Mr. Sloane) / $6.95

17251-5 PINTER, HAROLD / The Homecoming / $4.95

17885-8 PINTER, HAROLD / No Man's Land / $3.95

17539-5 POMERANCE, BERNARD / The Elephant Man / $4.25

17743-6 RATTIGAN, TERENCE / Plays: One / $5.95

17884-X STOPPARD, TOM / Travesties / $3.95

17260-4 STOPPARD, TOM / Rosencrantz and Guildenstern Are Dead / $3.95

17206-X WALEY, ARTHUR, tr. and ed. / The No Plays of Japan / $7.95

GROVE PRESS, INC., 196 West Houston St., New York, N.Y. 10014